GW00360952

Karen Kinney's second b
is such a gem. Reading it
most delicious chocolate
bites of her brilliant nuggets of wisdom were like the most
delicious, tantalizing, warmth-inducing shifts that melted
slowly in my soul. I felt myself awakening to a gentler,
more attentive, more intentional way of being in the world.
Doorways to Transformation had the effect of lifting veils
from my eyes.

—CATHERINE DEMONTE, psychotherapist and author of
*Beep! Beep! Get Out of My Way! Seven Tools for Powerful Creation
and Living Your Unstoppable Life*

Doorways to Transformation is a personal and expansive delve
into who we really are as creative beings. This book delivers
guidelines, inroads, and insights into everything from how
to grow still, to seeing clearly, to embracing the detours.

—TERRY PERSUN, award-winning novelist and poet

Doorways to Transformation gave me repeated opportunities
to take a deep breath, listen, reflect—and find just what
I needed to nurture my creative spirit. I felt as if I were
walking alongside a trusted friend. Karen has a way of
shifting our energy from worry to wonder. I love a book that
can do this—not only guide us, but remind us that our own
way of thinking sometimes needs a fresh perspective.

—MELISSA CISTARO, author of the award-winning memoir
Pieces of My Mother

This tender, insightful book is a welcome guide for creatives
and for anyone seeking to live more authentically. Karen
Kinney's gentle wisdom is a balm and a lodestar.

—AMY GOTTLIEB, author of *The Beautiful Possible*

In *Doorways to Transformation*, Karen Kinney brings clarity and conviction to the organic connection between creativity and spirituality. Each short chapter is a meditative moment, inviting us to pause, reflect, and bring inquiry to our own experiences. Writing as an expat, living in San Miguel de Allende, Mexico, Kinney brings fresh eyes and heartful insights to ordinary moments. With assurance, ease, and encouragement that comes from the depth of her lived experience, Kinney is a trustworthy guide along the path of living an authentic and integrated creative and spiritual life. This is the perfect book to live with, and to allow its wisdom to awaken our own wisdom.

—COLETTE LAFIA, international retreat leader, author of *The Divine Heart: Seven Ways to Live in God's Love*

Karen Kinney, in *Doorways to Transformation*, offers readers a compendium of gentle guidance for the artist within every one of us. Each chapter is a charming invitation to follow the author's hard-earned wisdom toward a richer, fuller expression of our creative selves.

—REV. DEBORAH MOLDOW, founder of the Garden of Light

If you are interested in manifesting an abundant, fulfilled life enriched by empathy and connectivity, Karen Kinney's book, *Doorways to Transformation*, is the perfect choice. It offers the reader a journey of gentle self-reflection alongside her own personal journey exploring the vibrant, warm culture and community of Mexico. After reading her book, you'll surely be gifted a new perspective—one ripe for cultivating freedom, joy, and peace.

—REBECCA LEFEBVRE, artist and author of *Within: Find Your Truth, Nourish Your Heart, Love Yourself*

Doorways to Transformation is lovely as a journey, very easy to read, intelligent, and engaging. I experienced magic from this offering and was deeply moved.

—RENE NORMAN, ceramicist, abstract painter, therapist in the healing arts

DOORWAYS TO
TRANSFORMATION

ALSO BY KAREN KINNEY

The Reluctant Artist:
Navigating and Sustaining a Creative Path

DOORWAYS TO TRANSFORMATION

Everyday wisdom for the creative soul

KAREN KINNEY

WINGED BIRD PRESS

Doorways to Transformation

Published by Winged Bird Press. Los Angeles, CA.

Cover design by Jo Walker
Interior design by Sea Script Company

www.karenkinney.com

ISBN (print): 978-0-9989395-2-0
ISBN (ebook): 978-0-9989395-3-7

First Printing, May 2022

Printed in the United States of America

WINGED BIRD PRESS

To all those on a contemplative journey of the heart

CONTENTS

Introduction 1

INTRODUCTION

*The larger the life you move into, the more you will be
called to trust in the Presence of a Love and Intelligence
that is beyond your linear mind. Your greatest desires
will call you to go where you have never been before.*
—TAMA KIEVES

This book is about the process of expansion. It is about
seizing all of who we are and daring to express it. It is
an offering of the soul—a manual for everyday spiritual
and creative growth—a celebration of the ordinary. It is
about pursuing transformative living and crafting a life
of meaning as we do.

Throughout this meditative guidebook, my desire is
to lead you on a journey of self-awareness and to encourage
you to think deeply about both your creative work and
your larger life. The principles and encouragement I
share have arisen from my own pursuit of transformation
and my journey as a professional artist and writer who
has engaged in creative practice and contemplative
spirituality for over twenty years. I also share insights I
have gleaned from being part of a community of writers,
musicians, and artists over the decades. Creative people
are natural observers, and my goal is to help you see
your daily reality in new ways.

On the following pages, you will encounter the marriage of creativity and spirituality in a context that extends beyond the craft of creating to address broader life experiences. Each chapter is designed to bring the energy of awakening into your day-to-day living and lead you to discover anew that all things are an opportunity for evolution, if we allow them to be.

The chapters are kept intentionally short in order to encapsulate a larger truth, idea, or deeper reality in a digestible form. Each one ends with prompts to elicit reflection. Use these prompts in the best way you see fit. Take them with you on a walk, journal about what you discover, or simply grow still and listen to what surfaces in response. Engage in the practice that most assists you in uncovering the gifts in the depths of your soul.

I have written the entirety of this book while living as an expat in Mexico, and I believe it is no accident that this particular work has been birthed in this country. For this offering needed a slow ripening—it was asking to be lived as it was written. And living cannot be sped up, as hard as we might try.

Through being immersed in a completely different cultural context, I have come to view life through another lens, one outside of the consumer-driven focus of the States. Mexican culture places greater value on the core of what truly matters—things like human connection, meaningful work, celebration, and faith. As a result, my own paradigms have shifted, resulting in a broader and richer spiritual worldview. I draw from this cultural influence to offer expanded insights into our own human metamorphosis.

In looking back, I can now see clearly that this has been a work of profound process. Mexico has allowed for and nurtured this unhurried maturation, and I hope you enjoy the beauty of another cultural thread woven throughout these pages.

The contemplations that ensue are succinct and gentle. It is not necessary to read them in a particular order, although I have given thought to the order in which they are placed. Listen to what you are drawn to and go there.

Above all, this is a book of wisdom. I hope it will provide a treasure trove of jeweled truths that bolster your creative work and your larger life. May its writing prompts and reflections lead you to an experience of inner freedom, joy, peace, and abundance.

1

TRANSITIONS

*Transitions. Crossing thresholds. Steps of faith. Releasing
what has come before as we cross the murky and undefined
landscape of in-between. The discomfort of temporary
spaces plants seeds of doubt. But I cannot ignore the vision
that beats in my heart; the potential I can sense is coming
as I believe for a future not yet realized. It has become
clear that a new container is required for growth.*
—JOURNAL ENTRY, APRIL 16, 2018

Ah, transition. It is not my strong suit, yet persevere I
must. Because good things await. How do I create from
this new energy source? I wonder. It is still so unfamiliar.
And I'm struggling to find my footing, feeling thrown
off track in my work. I remind myself that the steps to
create remain unchanged…simply choose to sit down
and do the work. Show up at the page. This makes sense.

I mull over these thoughts as I enter into my second
month of living in San Miguel de Allende, Mexico. So
many reasons inspired this move, including a long-
held desire to live internationally and an aspiration to
transition from an art career to writing and teaching—
work that feels even more aligned with my soul's
purpose. Getting to this point has been years in the

making, and I wonder if the second chapter of my life is beginning in this country. So much is new. Everything is, really.

Transitions are no easy feat. They challenge us at the core of our being, requiring us to become a lump of clay for a while—not yet here and not yet there. Some days I feel as if I am being forced into a lump of clay, as if there is no other option. Perhaps that is why I've been unable to shake my unsettled feelings and keep trying to define things ahead of schedule. The truth is, I am not good at being a lump of clay. I prefer the defined lines of planning and execution, and would prefer to bypass the gray areas that linger in between.

But ever so slowly, necessity is teaching me that it is okay to be not yet formed. Even though this grates against my nature, in reality I know that any passage from one thing to the next requires a period of venturing into the unknown. To cross its threshold, we must surrender what is familiar and be willing to journey through the darkness. And the only way out is through.

I remind myself once more to enjoy the journey and take comfort in knowing that the calling coming to me isn't in a hurry. Therefore, I don't need to be in a hurry. Pressure subsides as I exhale, allowing myself to more fully surrender to this great unknowing and its incubating darkness.

Transitions to something new often belie themselves with their enticing outward appearance. We forget that profound shifts are occurring underneath—things of substance that only reveal themselves over time. But this journey of allowing murky waters is a necessary prelude for what will follow, making the work of transition an integral time of laying the foundations for future growth.

I sit in a quiet nature preserve just outside of town and allow rest to overcome me as I let my head drop over my body. As I enter into this posture of relaxation, a small butterfly emerges from the grass and flies to a jagged rock a few feet away, vigorously beating its wings and finally growing still. This feels like a confirmation of my own surrender—my embrace of this glorious unknown.

As I observe the butterfly, I notice how it blends with its surroundings and is designed perfectly for this particular terrain. These thoughts ricochet back to my spirit, and I am graced with the awareness that I too am meant for this new land that I inhabit. I no longer need to see what my own lump of clay will become. There is a glory in life being unformed, one we so easily miss in our pursuit of "the next thing." The unknowing will work itself out in due time, paving the way for our own metamorphosis.

REFLECTIONS

- *How well do you navigate the murky waters of transition?*

- *Do you struggle with things being unformed in your life?*
- *How might these "lumps of clay" be invitations to welcome a passage into the unknown more fully?*

2
LIVING WITH "BOTH AND"

*Accept whatever comes to you woven in the pattern of
your destiny, for what could more aptly fit your needs?*
—MARCUS AURELIUS

My new life in San Miguel could not be more different
than my life in Los Angeles. LA is a massive city, full of
creative energy around every corner, and full of people.
The city's energy is coupled with a sense of expansiveness
and spaciousness in the ocean that borders it. Nature
along the California coastline provides a sense of calm
and peace that balances the chaos of the widespread
metropolis.

But yet, despite the masses of people living in close
proximity to one another, the city doesn't readily allow
for true connections. Although meeting people on a
surface level comes easily, a subtle sense of disconnection
penetrates relationships. As a result, life in LA contains
an emptiness that is hard to describe, something akin
to a heart longing. Busyness is coupled with a feeling
of isolation.

My experience in San Miguel is something entirely
different. It is a tiny town nestled in the hills in the

middle of Mexico, far from any coastline. Instead of being anchored by a large body of water, the town is full of stone—cobblestone streets and uneven sidewalks, stone churches and ancient buildings. One must travel outside of town to connect with nature, and even then, it is a desert-like and dry nature, far different from the oceanside living I've known for so many years.

Despite its much smaller size, San Miguel's streets are bustling and there is rarely a sense of isolation. Every morning when you step outside, you are greeted with a "buenos días" from every corner. Mexicans and expats alike are constantly connecting to one another, socializing and creating a strong sense of community. Emptiness is warded off by a profound sense of connection to the rest of humanity. Life is full in the ways that matter for the heart.

While it is easy to fall into compare and contrast mode amongst the places I've lived, searching for the one that feels most "complete," I realize this is an illusory quest. I am learning to embrace the "both and" in all of life, no matter where it takes me. Every geographic location I've ever lived in has shaped my soul in important ways. I am finally learning to walk in peace, regardless of circumstance.

The sense of stillness and spaciousness by the ocean in LA, its opportunities, and even the sense of isolation that pervades the city, coupled with the experience of heart-fullness and connectedness in a small, dusty Mexican town—each reality has transformed me in compelling ways. And, although it is human nature to wish for something that is missing in any situation, I'm realizing in new ways that the Divine is present in all of it. The good and the not-so-good—everything plays an integral role.

A "both and" mindset offers us an antidote to longing. It enables us to embrace the entirety of life and what it provides in each moment. Dorothy Hunt writes, "Peace is this moment without judgment—that is all. This moment in the heart-space where everything is welcome." How well do we receive the totality of all that our lives contain? Or do we find ourselves, instead, falling into wishful thinking, choosing an either/or kind of logic that keeps contentment just out of reach?

Each season refines a piece of our soul if we allow it to. Every experience has a transformative role to play, designed precisely for who we are at that particular moment in time. May this awareness aid us in living our lives from a place of greater acceptance and inclusivity.

REFLECTIONS

- *What seasons of your life have you resisted or wished were different in some respect?*
- *List a few ways (in retrospect) those seasons have touched and transformed your inner being.*

3

KINDNESS

Never underestimate the power of a single act of kindness.
—ZERO DEAN

It is July, and it is hot. The plants in my garden languish beneath the rays of the sun, and people on the streets carry umbrellas for shade. To escape the heat, I decide to venture out to a café for a cold drink. As I settle into a chair, the man at the next table accidentally bumps into mine. He apologizes profusely and then goes back to conversing with his wife and child.

A few moments later, he turns and, striking up a conversation, asks inquisitively where I am from. As I chat with him and his wife, I learn they are from Guadalajara and are visiting San Miguel as tourists for a few days. In a few weeks, they are headed to Ontario, California to visit extended family. When I tell him I am from Los Angeles, he jokes that LA is pretty much like Mexico, to which I laugh and agree. The conversation continues for a while as we discuss their family in the States and details about my time in Mexico. They ask how I am enjoying their country and sincerely welcome me as a foreigner multiple times, repeatedly remarking

12

that they hope I enjoy my stay. He ends by saying, *"You are truly welcome here."*

His last line leaves me taken aback, as I am unexpectedly moved by this display of sincere kindness. I can't help but think (with chagrin) how Spanish-speaking foreigners with very little English are so rarely welcomed in the same manner in many parts of the U.S. How often are kindness and gracious hospitality our first reaction to strangers from any part of the world?

This man's act of goodwill toward me models something significant for the divisions and conflicts we face in our world. His attempts to build a bridge give me hope that regular, everyday people can rally, repair, and create relationships, even when governments or institutions cannot. Even when injustices and walls seem to get the upper hand. Collectively, we can choose a different path—one marked by kindness, understanding, and connection.

To forge solidarity with whomever crosses our path is a powerful way to break down divisions and build a more hopeful future. What may appear like a simple act of kindness is never wasted, and in fact, has the capacity to leave us transformed.

REFLECTIONS

- *Have you ever been the recipient of unexpected kindness? How did it shift your perspective of the other person, your own situation, or the world?*

- *Think of one way you can show someone else an unexpected kindness this week.*

4

RIDING THE WAVE

Your inspiration is often waiting for you in the wild country of doing new things—not "thinking" about doing them. Jump in.
—TAMA KIEVES

Watching surfers follow the arc of a wave reminds me of how we experience both energetic and life shifts. In order to follow a new inspiration or direction, we must risk riding a force outside of ourselves, not knowing exactly where it is headed but trusting its crest and flow.

Living in accordance with our dharma, or our soul's purpose, inevitably requires us to ride waves that are increasingly in sync with our most authentic selves. This is both exhilarating and terrifying at the same time.

In anticipation of these transitions, we may find ourselves reverting back to old ways, relying on well-worn grooves and knowledge relevant to a past season. Although we may be quite aware that these ways of being and thinking no longer fit who we are, we are lured by the familiarity and the imagined sense of safety of already-lived places. Deep down we feel called to something new, but we are scared to follow the impulse.

But like the surfer and the wave, somewhere within each of us lies the ability to navigate the rise of a fresh flow. We are uniquely crafted to ride the particular wave that is calling our name, no matter how large it might appear. So we can either hunker down and willfully resist, choosing to remain in a past that no longer fits, or we can open ourselves up with a whole-hearted "yes" to the adventure that awaits.

Today I encourage you to follow what is beckoning. To free your spirit and release your hold on what is familiar and safe. You can't live into the possibilities of your future self if you are clenching too tightly to the past. Dive in. Your unique design is propelling you onward to an adventure you don't want to miss.

REFLECTIONS

- *Is there a new wave calling your name? What is one step you can take to dive in?*
- *Are there any "well-worn grooves" you are being called to surrender as you open yourself up to something new?*

5

GROWING CONFIDENCE

Don't think about making art, just get it done. Let everyone else decide if it's good or bad, whether they love it or hate it. While they are deciding, make even more art.

—ANDY WARHOL

Today, you have permission to celebrate your creative path—right now, in the present, no matter what your circumstances might look like or what goals may remain unreached. There is no need to wait until you are "farther along" or until your path is validated by others. You have the power to validate your work yourself. And at the end of the day, that is all that really matters.

The world frequently offers skewed definitions and a slow acceptance of who it considers to be *real* artists or *real* writers. It wasn't until I reached some of the bigger milestones in my art career, the flashier ones, so to speak, that various people said, in indirect ways, "Ah, now that you've done x, y, or z, we now recognize that what you do is the real deal. Your work is legitimate!" However, the work of creating is the same, whether you exhibit your creations in your bedroom, a local coffee shop, or at the Met. And it is the *act* of doing the work that makes you legit. You show up again and again. You trust the path. And as much as we might like to think otherwise, the end results are not in our control.

I'm at a beginning again, of sorts, in the midst of crafting a second creative career. This time, as a writer. Writing calls to me because it allows me to say things that I simply cannot say through art. It is a better tool for what I have to offer and express in this season of my life. And although it requires me to exit my comfort zone and embrace greater visibility, I must go where my creative instincts are leading.

I am no stranger to what it takes to build something from nothing. I've done it before and have confidence that I will do it again. But legitimizing your way isn't always easy in a world full of skeptics. And you are not alone in the struggle. I recently saw a documentary about acclaimed author Toni Morrison. In one of the interviews, she said that she couldn't fully call herself a writer until she had published her third book. Knowing who you are internally and proclaiming it to the world are two different things. And it can take time to get there.

So be patient with your creative efforts. For every dream you desire to pursue, remember to keep believing in your path, no matter the odds. It is yours and only yours to follow. Trust your vision. Your ability. Your power. Fully embrace the talent that lives within you. And never forget that the world needs what you alone have to offer. Your voice is one of a kind.

REFLECTIONS

- *In what ways can you encourage yourself to keep going on your creative path?*
- *Think of ways to acknowledge yourself each time you show up to do your work, no matter what goals remain unmet.*

6

UNEXPECTED ASSISTANCE

I do not at all understand the mystery of grace—
only that it meets us where we are but does
not leave us where it found us.
—ANNE LAMOTT

I leave for my morning's walk in an off mood. The construction workers began work next door at 8 a.m., and the music on their radio is turned up to accompany the banging. Since mornings are my best time for writing, the unbidden noise keeps me from digging into my work.

I start following my initial exercise route, but then decide to take a detour. I find myself walking up an incline that leads to the top of a hill overlooking large trees and the buildings below. Near the top, I discover a bench and, overcome by the tranquility and peace that surrounds it, decide to sit for a while and let my soul recenter.

When I resume exercising, I whisper an internal prayer for guidance in finding places of quiet refuge in our newly adopted town, which is normally a bustling hotbed of activity and noise. Silence and its many gifts are imperative companions for the creative work I do in the world. Silence assists me in growing still, accessing inner depths, and mining for gems to carry back to the surface.

As I ponder various solutions to the construction noise that has been going on for months, I imagine that something more drastic needs to happen, like finding a different rental in a quieter neighborhood, *right now*. Black-and-white change is the only obvious answer in my mind.

Walking back, I reflect on the unexpected silence that had been waiting for me on the bench overlooking the trees and the town. I recognize that it was a gift to rebalance my soul. Then, all of a sudden, a phrase drops into my thinking: "grace upon grace." And it hits me. Our circumstances will always have imperfections that beg to be adjusted. There is no escaping this reality of life. But perhaps the way we "fix" these imperfections comes through a greater awareness of the flow of grace that is presented to us each day. As we learn to recognize and accept these daily offerings of assistance, our outlook begins to change.

When I return home, I don't have my desired black-and-white solution of a different house far from any construction zone. But my soul has received the gift of silence on a hilltop bench.

Life will assist us in a myriad of subtle ways, if we are open to receiving. But many times, it is easier to get caught up in the seduction of big changes. Somehow, we think they promise us more. In believing this, we neglect to notice how our souls are being supported in our everyday circumstances. It is these less-noticeable sources of support that help us to shift and transform. They enable us to be at peace in the areas where life feels unresolved.

Expect these gifts of grace. Learn to search for them, and as you do you will see just how much is waiting to pour into your life. They might not always appear in the shiniest of outfits. But appear they will, and in just the form you need.

REFLECTIONS

- *In what subtle or unexpected ways has the Universe assisted you this week?*
- *Note especially the areas where you are feeling stuck, and see if you can find overlooked gifts of support.*

7

RECOGNIZING ALIGNMENT

*Your vision will become clear only when you look
into your heart. Who looks outside, dreams.
Who looks inside, awakens.*

—CARL JUNG

Years ago, I met an artist in Ojai, California who made an indelible impression on me. A ceramicist and painter, she lives on a ranch surrounded by green hills and trees. She is a physically beautiful woman, her hair a striking white and silver hue. And her insides are beautiful as well—her entire being radiates with peace and joy.

We initially met through social media after she expressed interest in some art materials I no longer needed. Ojai is a place I've traveled to occasionally for writing retreats, so on my next visit to the town, I got in touch about dropping off the supplies.

When I arrived at her studio, she offered me a hot cup of tea and we sat next to a huge picture window overlooking the trees on the hillside. We chatted about life, art, and the act of creating. She invited me to do an early morning hike the next day, and so I joined her just as the sun was starting to peek over the horizon. I remember walking in the crisp air, basking in the rays of light streaming over the hills. Flocks of birds soared overhead, and as we conversed, she seemed to be at one with the tranquil nature setting she calls home.

What struck me the most was how congruent her life appeared to be with her calling as a creative, contemplative soul. She wasn't spending time chasing things that weren't hers to pursue. She operated in a flow state, both taking aligned actions in the world and choosing to live in a location that supported what she was here on earth to do. Everything about her felt "in sync" with a larger, universal energy. Her countenance glowed, and I remember thinking that I wanted to be as in tune with my purpose in life as she was with hers.

Unfortunately, it is all too easy to become misaligned. We fall prey to others' agendas (and start to believe they are our own). We start accepting societal values that don't resonate with our soul's guidance. We become influenced by the subtle expectations of friends and family members that are not consistent with who we really are. Unaware of the power and value inherent in our true calling, we compare ourselves to others, envying a life that isn't ours to live. These are all forces that can deter us from our path.

But when we make the decision to live in accordance with our true Self, it shows. It is something that becomes palpable. We feel lit up inside, and even on the hard days we know that the work we are doing is what we are designed to do. As we courageously embrace our unique essence, we rise to our full height and cast other doubts aside. We finally recognize the difference between misguided paths and what is truly our own, and our countenance begins to reflect it. We are set on fire, and the world around us takes note.

REFLECTIONS

- *Where do you feel most aligned in life? Or, where and when do you feel lit up inside?*
- *Embrace these lit-up feelings as indicators of your core essence. Notice the settings, the kinds of work, and the relationships where you feel the most energy.*
- *What are some specific ways you can incorporate more of these things into your life?*

8

CELEBRATION

*Celebrate life in all its glory—challenge yourself
to let the routine sing and the new dance.*
—MAXIMILLIAN DEGENEREZ

The other weekend I traveled to Mexico City to visit a good friend. I stayed in my favorite neighborhood, which is filled with lush parks and tree-lined streets. Taking a walk is always a pleasure.

One afternoon, after sitting down on a park bench, I caught a glimpse of a man holding a gigantic mass of colorful balloons overhead—floating animals, stars, hearts, and yellow smiley faces. He walked through the park, calling out merrily as he went. Occasionally he stopped to play a toy flute, in the hopes of attracting either children or their parents to his colorful mass of delights.

Watching him pass by, a thought flickered through my mind—*This simple image of him captures so much of the true essence of Mexico, a country that excels at celebration, fun, and joy.* This is one of the reasons I find a lightness of spirit living here, something I am not so good at myself. With all its grown-up responsibilities, my adult persona feels the need to be more serious, and falls prey to the belief that she must work tirelessly toward accomplishments, making a constant effort to improve the world.

Maybe you can relate. In the midst of our endeavors, it can become second nature to carry all kinds of heavy responsibilities upon our shoulders. While not bad in and of themselves, they can easily sap a childlike joy and wonder from life.

But this balloon man and the gifts he carried invoked a sense of cheer within me. He elicited curiosity and aliveness. And he reminded me to celebrate. To treat life like a party far more often than I do. His presence suggested that our inner spirits come alive when we play. And that our creativity is nourished by celebration.

Sitting on my bench in the shade of a large tree, I felt grateful for the children at play and for the balloon man who encouraged their joy, lightness, silliness, and fun. One little boy ran excitedly down the path, a massive smile on his face, his giant balloon trailing behind him. His actions reminded me that celebration is a gift we can choose.

As I stood up to continue my stroll, I decided to take this precious child's example to heart and open myself a little more to wonder. Each day offers us a myriad of opportunities to consciously give welcome to delight.

REFLECTIONS

- *What deserves celebrating in your life?*
- *How can you allow a greater sense of wonder into the moments of your day?*

9

NURTURING PROCESS

The creative process is a process
of surrender, not control.
—JULIA CAMERON

When I first began writing years ago, I heard a respected teacher say it should never take anyone longer than ten months to write a book. I remember wondering if this was really true, and immediately thought of a fellow artist I know who took eight years to write his first book. And then I wondered how people come up with these seemingly arbitrary timelines.

External demands can easily squash our creative process, unless they are truly supporting the essence of a project. This isn't to say deadlines aren't helpful; they most certainly are. Most work doesn't get finished without one. But deadlines are often created without an awareness of what a project is trying to become and the time it will take to get there. Honoring process in our work means tuning into the nature of what is trying to be born.

As artists, we must learn to listen to our creations and not push them out too fast, nor keep them unexpressed for too long. Maintaining a steady rhythm of work helps us get in sync with the pace of any given project and allow for variation. When I wrote my first book, *The Reluctant Artist*, it was a very straightforward process. I felt that, in some ways, it had already been written before I officially started. Because so much of it already existed, whether in old blog posts, newsletters, or journal writing, my primary job was to compile material. Culling and organizing it fit with a tighter and shorter timeline. The process felt pretty well-defined.

This book is turning out to be a much more organic journey, and it feels as though I am living the content as I am writing it. Thus, by default, the timeline is both longer and looser. For the act of living is, of course, not something that can be stuffed into a neat package. Whereas my first book was more left-brain, this one is more right-brain, and it has become quite clear that something entirely different wants to be born this time around.

We enjoy our creativity more when we stop judging a project's particular rhythm and, instead, get in sync with what it wants to be. As we listen, we learn that every creation has an identity. And when we allow for process, adjusting expectations and outcome accordingly, we nurture these unique identities. We liberate our art from a cookie-cutter mold.

REFLECTIONS

- *In what ways do external demands derail the process of your art?*

- *How can you surrender more fully to your creativity, allowing it to flourish in a manner consistent with its identity?*

10

THE JOURNEY OF BECOMING

The world around us is nothing more and nothing less than a mirror of what we have become from within.
—GREGG BRADEN

Geographic moves always prompt growth in me. A new environment requires me to learn a way of being that fits a different context. Changed surroundings beautifully nurture these fresh ways of being. As they take root, they facilitate our next wave of transformation—our next "becoming," so to speak.

However, these changes are not always easy to embody. I struggled with this when I first moved to Los Angeles. The entire city exudes a creative vibe that, over time, became an integral part of my evolution. However, the energy in LA encourages more of an organic adaptation to career opportunities—one that allows the work you are doing to grow serendipitously instead of forcing a pre-existing box around it. This is quite different from the more traditional, regimented approach to work I was accustomed to in the Midwest. Figuring out how to adjust to this different reality and flow was foundational to my becoming an artist, and I learned how to live and work in ways previously foreign to me. Much of my structured, more-linear thinking had to be released to allow for this change to come about.

Learning an unfamiliar way to see, experience, or live in the world requires us to adopt a beginner's mindset and release old paradigms. Our ego usually protests this at first, for it prefers clear parameters, certainty, and established ways of doing things. But, if we desire to keep evolving throughout our lives, we must be willing to try on new ways of being that foster our own growth.

In recent days, I've been wondering just how Mexico will elicit a new way of being within me and what learning curve it will facilitate. Its culture encourages a completely different way of engaging with life than the States'. I'm still learning what this is, feeling my way into unfamiliar territory, contrasting cultural influences and divergent ways of engaging with my surroundings.

But I can't help but think that the distinct way of being I will learn to embody here is inextricably tied to the next becoming calling my name. I can feel my identity reaching toward this next wave of transformation as it beckons from the horizon. And on my best days, I am learning to surrender to its unmistakable current and rhythm, knowing that it is an integral part of my future growth.

REFLECTIONS

- *What evolution or life shift are you in the midst of?*
- *In what ways will adopting a beginner's mindset assist you in your own becoming?*
- *What paradigms from your past do you need to release?*

11

THE VALUE OF REST

*Life is not a burden to carry. My actions don't 'count' more
if they weigh more. Quite the opposite. It is in lightness of
foot that I reach the heights to which I am meant to climb.
It is in freedom of movement and joy in my soul that I
bring forth my purest and most powerful essence. In rest,
I remember that all will come forth in due time.*
—JOURNAL ENTRY, OCTOBER 10, 2018

Creators need to rest. This might feel counterintuitive in a world that is always "on." Rest, after all, isn't allowed when making tangible outcomes is the only measure of progress, right? Far from it. When we remember that what we create is equivalent to giving birth, rest takes on an entirely new relevance.

Rest is not a departure from production; rather, it is the seedbed of germination. Rest is when our souls get filled up and come alive again, and new ideas sprout forth. Rest is permitting our inner artist to come out and play. Rest is allowing enough stillness in our days to hear prompts for our next direction. In rest, we lay the foundations for our next creative visions.

Some of the best ideas surface when we are not consciously pushing our creative work forward, and instead, purposely allow moments of seeming nothingness. These ideas come in the shower, as we daydream and look out the window, when we take a meandering walk, or when we doodle on a piece of paper. *Whenever we suspend agenda,* these moments feed our souls and nurture our art. They are vital interludes in bringing our dreams to fruition.

Innovation comes from rejuvenation. So don't be afraid of rest in a 24/7 world. Your body, mind, and spirit will thank you. And most important, so will your creations.

REFLECTIONS

- *What does rest look like for you?*
- *How is your creative soul best replenished?*
- *How can you practice suspending agenda?*

12

FINDING YOUR VOICE

*Each one of us has the power to create an energetic
vibrancy through our personal expression that impacts
everything. That's how we begin to change the world.
We heal one person at a time, and we start with ourselves.*
—DEBRA SILVERMAN

How do we find our voice? Some people are born with
a natural proclivity to speak. These people are the per-
formers, the ones energized in front of a crowd, rarely at a loss for words. Inner musings flow forth easily.
Others of us choose our words with more apprehension,
remaining silent as someone else's voice fills the space or
shaping our thoughts into what we think those around
us wish to hear.

It is quite easy to speak what we have been conditioned to say, allowing our inmost selves to remain
hidden in exchange for a dialogue with an external
stamp of approval. It is the rare soul who dares to pursue authenticity, willing to speak their truth without
self-censorship, and feeling comfortable doing so. Not
many take the journey required to find the voice of
their soul. It is an excavation that takes time and in-

tention—one that necessitates a willingness to shift and grow.

My dear friend labored under the guise of the voice that others expected of her for years. She studied hard to become a medical doctor, fulfilling her family's expectations of what success looked like. And she worked as a pediatrician for over a decade. Although she was well-paid, she never felt truly called to the work she was doing. Every day, she felt like she was playing a role for which someone else was better suited. And her *real* voice, the one that only her closest friends knew, remained buried.

It wasn't until midlife that she decided to begin her own excavation process and uncover what was genuinely calling to her. She eventually took the plunge and built a new business as a relationship coach, helping others work through the challenges inherent in finding a soul partner. This venture was a stark departure from the particular voice (and financial success) she had been conditioned to pursue, and it took time, courage, and persistence. But eventually, she carved out a new niche for herself—running workshops, speaking at seminars, and doing one-on-one coaching. For the first time in her life, she felt she was using her voice in the way it was meant to be used in the world. She experienced a profound level of liberation and freedom.

But getting to this point was not an easy journey. My friend had to leave behind what others expected of her and trust that it was safe to reveal her authentic voice—the one that filled her with life and with passion. She had to take the risk of rebranding her work and her image to reflect her heartfelt desires, and she had to engage in self-examination to find the right words to match her inner evolution.

Similarly, my own journey to find my voice has been just as winding. I certainly did not start out in a career that mirrored who I really am inside. It took me years to find my true calling: that of a creative soul—a contemplative writer, artist, and teacher. And I needed to exert further effort to learn how to boldly share that voice with others instead of keeping it shrouded in self-doubt and uncertainty.

If you have ever lived in ways that have masked, distorted, or hidden your real self from view, take heart. Know that you do not need to resign yourself to an obscured reality. It is not only possible to excavate the core of who you are, but it may, in fact, be a significant part of your life's work. As Stephen Cope writes in his book, *The Great Work of Your Life*, "It is better to fail at your own dharma than to succeed at the dharma of someone else." In essence, there is great reward in the effort to unshackle our innermost identity, regardless of the outcome. It is possible and desirable that we liberate the voice that wants to speak—the one that needs to be heard by those around us.

This transformation will not happen overnight. It will require us to explore, follow our intuition, probe into our depths, and take uncomfortable risks. But the alternative, living a life that does not reflect our deepest selves, binds us to a false existence that robs us of our gifts.

Discovering, honing, and sharing your authentic voice is vital work, and there is unfathomable power in speaking the truth that is only yours to speak. It is a power worth cultivating.

REFLECTIONS

- *Where are you on the journey of finding and living your most authentic self?*
- *How strongly do you believe that your voice has the power to transform the lives of those around you?*

13

ALLOWING EASE

*Sometimes people are simply afraid to pursue
something that seems to come so easily to them—
shouldn't success be difficult? No, it shouldn't.*
—MARK VICTOR HANSEN

Oftentimes our best progress comes through noticing what is easy. But instead of simply allowing what comes most naturally, we fall prey to thinking we need to make our art or music or writing really *hard*. We believe that increased difficulty is somehow a sign that we're on the right path. If we're not sweating enough, something is amiss, right? This certainly fits the American mantra of "no pain, no gain." But is this actually true? Sometimes all pain leads to is more pain. And we end up worn out, exhausted, and wondering what went wrong.

Furthermore, "relaxing" is often construed as a dirty word. But when we relax, we let go of tension. We become more moldable and responsive and begin to trust our instincts. Our areas of gifting always express themselves quite effortlessly from this relaxed state, if we take care to support and nurture them. We are made precisely for what we love the most. And as we learn to relax into our gifts and embrace what comes most readily, we evolve into our creative selves with far less pain and far more grace.

The truth is, we are being supported and guided by a loving Universe. This support comes to us in countless ways every day. But it is often overlooked, because the guidance we receive feels too obvious, or somehow too simple. *Real progress must be complicated and hard,* we tell ourselves. And so surely this thing that comes so easily to me, or this step I'm being prompted to take that is totally within my reach couldn't *really* count, could it?

But what if our only job on our journey of evolution is to say *yes* to our essence? And what if the weight of our becoming isn't actually on us? What if, instead, we are being invited to walk a path of ease. To trust and not doubt. And to assume that there is ample provision, sufficient time, and plentiful resources available. Perhaps then we can move from the "no pain, no gain" mantra to having faith that each natural and even pleasurable step forward will lead us exactly where we need to go at just the right time.

REFLECTIONS

- *Do you find yourself overlooking things that come easily to you?*
- *Do you give more value to difficulty or define progress only by how much you labor?*
- *Start to observe how places of ease assist you in moving forward.*

14

BLOOMING

*Life is created when you trust in the promise of unseen
things, just as buds hold life in the depth of winter.*
—SISTER STANISLAUS KENNEDY

A friend of mine began this year with great anticipation.
Several opportunities to advance her career opened up,
she was considering moving to a new location she had
long dreamed about, and a romantic relationship had
entered her life, promising good things for the future.
She said to me on a phone call one day, "I'm blooming!"
And it was true. She was blooming, and everything in
her life was mirroring this same reality back to her.

Then, things shifted. At least in the outer world.
Opportunities that had appeared to be open doors were
put on hold. Her upcoming move was delayed because
her mom got sick. And the new business she was starting
needed to be postponed because her business partner
backed out. In essence, life happened. The excitement
and momentum she'd experienced at the start of the
year began to fade away.

If she was honest, she knew she was experiencing
only temporary setbacks. Temporary pauses. But one

day amid these delays, she wondered, "Is my life still blooming?" She had felt this reality so strongly at the beginning of the year. And now, her vision was cloudy.

She loves to spend time in her garden, and each time she observed her growing plants, they never failed to offer encouraging insights. (Nature has an uncanny way of mirroring principles of growth that we often forget.) In her yard, there is a catalpa tree. It is always the last tree to leaf out in the springtime, and its flowers take even longer to appear, not arriving until summer. She had always been curious about why its blossoms took such a long time to emerge. But when they did come, they were the most spectacular ones in the garden and they filled the yard with a beautiful scent. Their blooming was worth waiting for.

After observing her catalpa tree for a while, my friend shared the realization that dawned on her: *If something is beginning to bloom, then we can trust that nature will finish its cycle and allow it to fully bloom. Even and especially when the blooms are taking much longer to appear than we might prefer.*

Each tree and flower knows exactly when to bloom and how to bloom, and so it is with our lives. Your next evolution knows when it needs to emerge and how it will look and be in the world. But when life around us begins to press in, we can easily forget what nature makes so abundantly clear, and we lose sight of what we were so sure of just moments before.

The catalpa tree reminded my friend that she is still in the blooming season she felt so strongly at the beginning of the year. The detours she was encountering didn't make that any less true. They just required her to embrace greater patience, along with a fuller surrender of when the promising new blossoms in her life would come forth. But come forth they would. The buds that had begun to grow would become manifest in due time.

When we set our energies toward our life pursuits, we too can trust that they will unfold. Our intentions are what have set their growth in motion. Our job is to trust their timeline and remember that every cluster of buds will eventually turn into full blooms. Nature always knows the course to take.

REFLECTIONS

- *Where do you see new buds forming in your life?*
- *Has their growth appeared to come to a standstill, or do you find yourself doubting they will reach maturity?*
- *Consider how you can rest anew in what nature mirrors to us—once a growth cycle has begun, it will be completed.*

15

TRUSTING DESIRE

*The heart, then, becomes a reliable guide for
decision making. We can trust our hearts'
desires, for they speak of our truest essence...*

—JOURNAL ENTRY, NOVEMBER 14, 2017

Desire is one of the most sacred forms of guidance we
can receive. And no one reminds me of this truth more
than a powerful life coach and speaker named Tama
Kieves. I first discovered Tama years ago on Facebook
and signed up to receive her daily inspirational quotes
of life wisdom. They impacted me so much that I even
thought of sharing my own writing and teaching in
a similar fashion. Then I rediscovered what I already
know—that my personal rhythm and creative flow
emerges in a more seasonal fashion than a regular,
everyday digest.

Nevertheless, she is a writer who continually af-
firms for me the importance of our desires, or what I
call "glimmers of life." Too often we're taught to distrust
these glimmers, or what, in essence, is an innate guidance system, and encouraged instead to let "shoulds" or
obligations drive our path. But the problem with living

an obligated life is that it doesn't awaken us to real life. And though we're created to be fully alive during this journey on the planet, we settle for what is numb, mechanical, or expected.

Tama wisely writes, "We are given our dreams and desires for a reason. They are the portals to inspired living. It's our work to choose this life. It's our work to choose to believe we're called by something Alive to be exceptionally alive, to answer that call...with ten thousand actions of love, courage, and gratitude."

Following our unique glimmers of life does indeed require love, courage, and gratitude. We must first learn to embrace ourselves and everything planted within us. As we replace self-judgment with acceptance, we allow ourselves to welcome all we are meant to become. Then we must harness boldness to take leaps of faith, for pursuing any spark of life will entail some measure of risk. And walking in gratitude is what will allow us to uncover our desires in the first place. Thankfulness has a knack for illuminating the places where our souls naturally sing.

John O'Donohue wrote, "May I have the courage today to live the life that I would love, to postpone my dream no longer, but do at last what I came here for." The next time you feel the seeds of a desire begin to take root, resist any hesitation that might try to dampen its growth. Instead, receive it as a sacred guidepost whispering your name. Follow it. Love it. And risk taking a dive into the life for which you are designed.

Trust that desire will help lead you to your soul's true home.

REFLECTIONS

- *What makes your soul sing? Where, when, and with whom do you feel most alive?*
- *What is one brave step you can take to move toward your desires?*

16

GIVING OURSELVES RECOGNITION

If we never stop to recognize our progress, we will
be forever tethered to an unrelenting treadmill
of dissatisfaction. It is only in feeling proud
of who we are today that we experience
lasting contentment in our soul.
—JOURNAL ENTRY, JANUARY 28, 2019

One of the downsides of living in a Mexican colonial town is the wildly uneven cobblestone streets that make walking (or any other form of exercise) extremely challenging. I've gained an entirely new appreciation for flat concrete as a result. In Los Angeles, my exercise route for years was a paved bike path along the ocean. Toward the end of my time in California, I started trekking up into the hills that surround the city. In many ways, my switch to hiking the hillside was symbolically parallel to my upcoming relocation to Mexico—I was ready for new terrain and new vistas to explore.

Now, most days, even though I have traded wooded hills for rocky streets, I still feel like I am hiking. This morning, as I navigate the cobblestones, continually looking down to avoid misstepping or twisting my ankle, I marvel at how adept I have become at traversing such uneven terrain. It almost feels like I have mastered some sort of extreme sport!

Any time we are plunged into a different setting, no matter how foreign, we have no choice but to learn new skills. And we end up becoming accomplished at all kinds of things, possibly even surprising ourselves with the types of proficiencies we acquire. In the midst of our learning, there is tremendous value in pausing once in a while to appreciate just how far we've come. No matter how big or small our achievements, taking time to acknowledge how much we've grown and how well we've adapted to new challenges is essential to our soul's well-being.

Today, instead of looking for your next growth curve or mountain to climb, try celebrating instead. Affirm yourself for having grasped something unfamiliar. For adapting. For overcoming the latest wrench thrown into your path. Take time to stop and recognize your own evolution in the midst of life's journey.

While becoming all we are meant to be, it behooves us to pause and feel satisfied with who and where we are at this moment in time. In validating how much we have overcome, grown, and learned, we gain a fresh appreciation for all that we embody.

REFLECTIONS

- *How much do you appreciate who you are in the present? How can you recognize and celebrate how far you've come?*

- *Think of five ways you have grown over the past several months or years that make you especially proud.*

17
RESISTING URGENCY

Above all, trust in the slow work of the Spirit. We are quite naturally impatient in everything to reach the end without delay. Let your ideas mature gradually—let them grow. Let them shape themselves, without undue haste.
—PIERRE TEILHARD DE CHARDIN

The siren call of urgency. It's what fuels our days in a capitalistic, money-making society. In a society fixated on externals, speed, and production. At its root, this pull toward urgency originates from a belief in scarcity. If there's not enough for everyone, then we must secure our piece before it's gone. And quickly. Moving slowly is equated with missing out.

We experienced this sense of urgency from numerous angles, all in 48 hours this past weekend. We wanted to look at a house we were interested in purchasing and made an appointment for Friday at noon. The house had not even come on the market. A realtor friend informed us of the listing, telling us to get ahead of everyone else by taking advantage of an early sneak peek.

After viewing it, we were interested enough to consider making an offer. Our own realtor told us she knew of another buyer prepared to pay all cash for it on Saturday, so if we were serious, we'd need to make an offer Friday evening. Faced with this time pressure, we went home to discuss it and ended up putting an offer in before going to bed.

We had a restless night, doubting and wondering if we'd made the right decision. The following morning, we received an "offer to buy" document to sign and were given three days to return it. Still uncertain, we were grateful for a few days to process its actuality more thoroughly. But after just one day, the seller's agent said that unless we signed the document within a few hours, the purchase agreement would no longer be valid. As fate (or luck) would have it, my husband was traveling that day and was unreachable. Unable to confirm a final decision with him, we chose to let the property go.

In reflecting on the experience, I realized that every single party, from the realtor who sent the listing before it came on the market to our own realtor who showed us the property to the seller's agent, had used language designed to communicate a belief in scarcity. Phrases like *"There won't be another house like this one"* and *"If you don't act now, you'll regret it."* Hence, speed became paramount.

Of course, this artificially created belief in scarcity is what drives sales. But it is fascinating to ponder how much of our lives are driven by an urgency that's based on an illusion (in this case, the illusion that there couldn't possibly be another house that would meet our needs equally well).

When we recognize this illusion for what it is, it becomes possible to choose a different reality and adopt a worldview that isn't dominated by rushing. Seeing through the illusion of scarcity helps us to slow down and embrace the truth that a higher order is orchestrating life in a way that makes "missing out" a misnomer.

The reality we choose to believe is the one that the world will reflect back to us. When we focus on a sense of lack, we start experiencing anxiety and feel the need to grasp anything that passes by, fearful that there won't be another. But when we learn to relax and trust that what is meant for us will flow to us (and that what isn't is not something to be missed), we will be more discerning with our choices.

If we were to release urgency and the scarcity mindset that propels it, how might it shift our days? How would it alter our actions and shape our hearts? I believe that gratitude would become more prominent. Instead of seeing a world of lack, we would see the glass as being half full. Our actions would be fueled by peace instead of driven by fear. And our hearts would beat more confidently. We would know that our fear of missing out is simply an illusion that keeps us from seeing the truth of all that is available.

When we resist the siren call of urgency, we discover that rushing does not actually get us ahead, and we permit ourselves to align with the flow of life.

REFLECTIONS

- *What is your response to your own fear of missing out? Is it one of surrender and trust, or do you find yourself propelled into anxiety and grasping for straws?*
- *What is one way you can practice resisting a false sense of urgency?*

18

ABUNDANCE

Abundance is now, not somewhere in the future.
It's waiting for you to simply step into it.
—JOURNAL ENTRY, APRIL 3, 2018

Recognizing abundance in the universe is first and foremost an act of being present. How many times do we suspend our contentment by attaching it to a future event? We say things like, well, when this happens, or that happens, *then* I will be happy, or *then* my life will look as it should. Our future-minded thoughts, though perhaps well intentioned, rob us of the flow that is available to us right now, and in fact, is only available now. In our attempts to strain for the future, we end up missing the opportunity to dive into wells of abundance that are only given in the moment.

My French writer friend just had $100 worth of alcohol delivered to her house today. She and her husband were joking about stocking up on needed supplies after being quarantined for two months during the COVID-19 pandemic. They were enjoying exploring mixology and making fancy cocktails in the evenings as a new creative outlet.

She relays this news to me on the very morning I sit down to write this chapter on abundance. And I realize that this action is a perfect illustration of seeing the reality of an abundant universe even in the midst of great lack. Instead of focusing on all the things taken away during the pandemic (gathering with others, economic stability, etc.), she is celebrating the fact that a service exists that will deliver a wide variety of alcohol to one's home, and in great quantity, no less!

Although this may appear to be a small thing, abundance more often than not comes to us in glimpses instead of a massive tidal wave. It is why we must train our eyes to see it. We literally need new vision to help us tune in to an energetic field of provision, instead of one of deficit. We have the power to shift both our perception of reality and our subsequent experience of that same reality.

On a recent trip to a park, I sat down on a bench overlooking multiple waterfalls cascading over a rocky precipice. I reclined, my legs stretched out in front of me, and took in the view, relishing the sound of the rushing water. The waterfalls were the epitome of a never-ending supply. And as I sat there observing, I wondered to myself, *What if we were to believe that there is an infinite supply always being poured out toward us? Would this increase our awareness of abundance, and even more so, our ability to receive it?*

Simply put, where we let our minds dwell matters. We can entertain anxious assumptions about a felt lack we must strive to fix. Or we can look for the evidence that supports a deeper truth—that we are being cared for by a loving Universe, even and especially in times when our circumstances send us messages to the contrary. An abundance lens assists us in seeing the synchronicity that is trying to come our way, precisely when we are most in need.

It is not a matter of whether the synchronicity is there or not—it is a matter of our own receptivity. When we open up to receive, we begin to see exactly how we are being provided for and can more easily trust that a way will be found, no matter what obstacles are on the path. Abundance isn't a word to simply describe when all appears to be going well. It is more a reality of the universe that is there to ground us in the here and now, no matter what life happens to be serving up at the moment. Ultimately it is the belief that our needs are being met— not tomorrow, nor next week—but in the very present moments of today.

REFLECTIONS

- *What are some ways your present reality reflects an abundant universe?*
- *Identify a current circumstance where you are experiencing a sense of lack and try viewing this situation through a lens of abundance instead. Ask yourself, "How are my needs being met, despite the challenges I am facing?"*

19

TRUE CONNECTION

Connection: The energy that exists between people when they feel seen, heard, and valued; when they can give and receive without judgment; and when they derive sustenance and strength from the relationship.
—BRENÉ BROWN

My Mexican artist friend returns from New York City with a dejected look on her face. "Connection was so difficult there," she bemoans. Tales of people glued to their phones follow, and then an idea for an art exhibition that would examine the concept of connection and disconnection in the age of technology.

I can relate 100 percent to what she shares. Large cities can be very lonely places. They give the appearance of community, what with the millions of people that inhabit them and swarm their streets. But actual face-to-face time easily gets usurped by people's technology addictions and the ubiquitous option to check out.

Personal development blogger Matthew Mueller writes, "Technology and the everyday hustle has made us socially distant and immune to true connection, mistaking mere acquaintances with connection. We get more neurological stimulation from a 'like' or a notification than we do from a passerby saying 'hello.'"

Technology and its isolating effects are everywhere. But I find them buffered living in Mexico, simply because Mexican culture places an extremely high value on face-to-face time. As is true in most Latin American countries, relationships are the primary currency for everything. Actual in-person, daily interactions are how things get accomplished, in a nuanced, extensive network that exists outside of most technology channels.

As a result, getting anywhere takes time. A simple walk to run some errands isn't just a walk to run some errands. I'll pass my neighbor, who I must stop to chat with (not doing so is considered rude). Then a few blocks later I might run into a friend or acquaintance. At the tienda, I know the shopkeeper and take time to exchange pleasantries. Getting from point A to point B is never a straight line. It is a curving path, and time must be allowed for the relational detours that arise.

This in-depth, relational currency is much more time-consuming than surface online exchanges. It requires showing up somewhere, taking time to talk to people, and being much more present to your surroundings. But it is by far more rewarding. You come to *see* people in entirely new ways and gain the riches of intimacy on a different level.

We lose something profound when efficiency becomes our primary goal. Technology, of course, aids this fixation with efficiency and seems to replace real-life interactions with greater and greater frequency. But the truth is, we are relational beings, and when real-life relationships get crowded out by a screen, people's spirits suffer.

So, instead of fixating on the online world, these days I'm making a decided effort to let my energy be captured by the real world and all it offers. This is where meaningful life is happening. In our search to connect, we would be well-served by taking an honest look at how our devices rob us of what is real, and examining how often we exchange relational richness for an illusion of closeness. With minimal effort, we can begin to prioritize who and what is in front of us and watch life grow fuller as a result.

REFLECTIONS

- *Do you feel deeply connected to others? If not, what are some ways you can incorporate in-person exchanges into your weekly rhythm?*
- *Consider fasting from technology for a day and see what kinds of real-world conversations open up as a result.*

20

CREATING SPACE

Create space for what really matters.
—JEN RIDAY

I am beginning this chapter as the coronavirus pandemic enters its second year. People worldwide are struggling with so many things—health, finances, social isolation, and job loss. The challenges in this era are numerous. But from the beginning of the outbreak, many of us took on an unnecessary challenge. We prioritized our need for life to continue at the same pace and productivity level that it always has. This impulse reveals our discomfort with less. Less busyness. Less commotion. Less noise. We struggled with the reality of our days and weeks slowing way down and scrambled to fill in the void any way we could.

I've received more Zoom invitations in the past few weeks than I have in my whole life. I am oversaturated! I had hoped to spend the enforced quarantine in increased times of contemplation to create a more voluminous container for all kinds of inspired writing to pour forth. This is still my goal, but I'm finding it is becoming much harder to achieve than I imagined. Instead of in-person gatherings being temporarily on hold, they are all being converted to online meetings. The pace of life must continue! And I'm not referring to necessary economic activity related to employment and commerce. I'm referring to everything else—exercise classes, yoga classes, writing groups, spiritual meetings, recreational groups, book clubs, etc.

Granted, some of these online meeting conversions are worthy attempts to ward off social isolation. But I see this frantic switch of everything moving online as going beyond that. It's almost like we are uncomfortable with unoccupied time. We are unable to embrace silence. We are reluctant to decrease our activity level, for fear of what thoughts or emotions or disquieting moments of self-awareness might spring forth. Or maybe we simply fear boredom. As a culture, we have an addiction to activity. We are predisposed to busyness and to life being unduly full. And in the absence of that full feeling, something strikes us as amiss.

Consumeristic cultures have a difficult time with the concept of margin. But perhaps this is one of the things we need most: to counter and begin healing our addiction to operating at top speed every hour of the day. Instead, we can intentionally create space and allow it to shift our priorities and feed our souls.

Crises do not come without gifts. And one of the great gifts of a pandemic that forced the entire world inside is the opportunity to embrace a greater sense of spaciousness in our lives. Increased margin offers us a chance to learn to be with ourselves in a more honest way than we may have been in years. It invites us to listen to everything that is surfacing and to experience, possibly for the first time, the life-enhancing benefits of less freneticism.

Nourishment often comes in unexpected ways. Let's not miss the invitation to let go of the pull of our overly scheduled lives and choose a different rhythm instead.

REFLECTIONS

- *Are you uncomfortable with space in your life?*
- *In what ways have you bought into the cultural norm that more and busy are optimal?*
- *What are some ways you can shift your day-to-day activities to create room for what you find most meaningful?*

21

LIFE-GIVING MOVEMENT

Where is life flowing? Follow it. Nothing ever needs to be made to happen, or forced. Jump into the river and trust its movement. It will bring you all the gifts you need.
—JOURNAL ENTRY, JUNE 22, 2018

When I first moved to Mexico, I heard the above words in my spirit very clearly. And they were followed by this: *"Enjoy flowing in the river on this trip, not climbing a treadmill. Both allow for forward movement."*

While the "trip" turned into a multi-year stay, this instruction has continued to prove helpful as I explore a new culture. I am well accustomed to moving forward; it is one of my strengths. But in American culture, we are often taught to move forward with brute strength, grit, or sheer force. I compare forward movement in America to climbing a steep treadmill. Great exertion is required and the goals we are moving toward are always "out there," just beyond reach.

Conversely, flowing in the river is more about attunement. It is the skill of attuning our lives, our energy, and our actions with what is already forming and wants to come forth. Mexican culture encourages and values flowing in the river much more than its neighbor to the north. A deep-seated acceptance is woven into the fabric of life. And this acceptance supports a posture of flowing as opposed to force.

I've often wondered why more people don't choose the way of the river, myself included. Maybe it is because this kind of movement requires greater surrender. It necessitates relinquishing control over what direction you travel and how fast you go. Flowing in the river ushers us into an embrace of mystery. It teaches us to partner with the energy surrounding us and to abdicate the role of dictating outcomes. Flexibility becomes more important than strength. As a result, our actions and movements become less rigid and begin to harmonize with a larger unfolding. Our part is simply learning to discern it.

Climbing a treadmill or flowing in the river—both allow for movement. But these days, I am finding the latter to be the most life-giving for my soul.

REFLECTIONS

- *Do you feel the need to use force to climb to new heights? Try attuning to the movement of life around you instead and see what changes you notice in your soul.*
- *Identify one thing in your life that's flowing easily.*

22

FOSTERING SAFETY

*Grant yourself the experience of safety
you need in order to grow.*
—ANONYMOUS

This morning as I write, our adopted cat has chosen to lie down directly next to me, *almost* on my lap but not quite, nuzzling up against my right leg. In order to preserve the moment, I do my best to not move, and am cognizant of the fact that this is close to a divine miracle.

We adopted Sophie nine months ago from the local animal shelter. And to say she was skittish when we first got her would be a vast understatement. She spent the first three months hiding under the bed, only coming out for occasional food and water. Very slowly (emphasis on *very*), she has started to venture into the open, taking risks like sleeping in plain sight or daring to let us pet her without running away. She has even begun to sit "next" to me on the couch, but usually at least five feet away.

You can imagine my surprise when, today, she decided to jump up and nestle right against my body as

I am working. I revel in this rarity and begin to wonder if one day, most likely far into the future, she might even decide to sit on my lap.

As I intermittently write and contemplate our cat, I realize that here is a simple yet profound life lesson staring me in the face. And it has to do with safety and the time it takes us to learn it. For we can be skittish creatures too. We try dipping our toes into something and then pull back. We open up in a relationship and then retreat when our sharing isn't reciprocated. We try a new skill and then wonder if we can really master it when it doesn't come easily on the first go. We hear a creative instinct inside but then drop it, afraid that it might be too "out there."

Opening up to life and growth is risky business. And the process to enter new territory doesn't come wrapped up in a tidy package with guaranteed results. On the contrary, it is quite messy and asks us over and over again to trust. But trust isn't something that is learned overnight.

Therefore, our own steps outside of our comfort zone need to be met with great levels of patience, gentleness, and affirmation. We can offer these gifts to ourselves as often as we need them, and by doing so, create conditions of safety that support our risk-taking. As we grow in confidence, our feelings of safety will eventually grow with us.

For months, I doubted whether Sophie would

ever show us any affection at all. And very, very slowly, inch by inch, she is proving me wrong. She is a living example that trust *can* be learned, no matter what scary or disappointing experiences you've had in the past. With practice, a sense of safety will grow over time, taking you beyond what previously felt impossible.

REFLECTIONS

- *What are you afraid of right now?*
- *In what ways can you grant yourself an experience of safety as you try something new?*

23

ENCOURAGING EXPLORATION

Sometimes the most scenic roads in life are the
detours you didn't mean to take.
—ANGELA BLOUNT

A musician friend I admire is extraordinarily goal-oriented and has a keen ability to produce a very particular style of music. She frequently draws on her left brain to create structure around her work and achieve the milestones she sets for herself. But she often tells me that she struggles to break out of the product box she has created. Every time she attempts something totally new, she encounters resistance.

It can be satisfying to check off the creative goals we set for ourselves. But operating in a focused production mode for too long leaves very little time for actual exploring. We forget to abandon structure and let our right brain come out to play. My last few years living in Los Angeles fell more along these lines. The projects I had lined up required extreme output and had somewhat rigid timelines. On the plus side, I adopted a single-minded focus and achieved some great things, but I didn't have much space for growing or expanding beyond them.

Conversely, I'm finding the creative energy in my current season of life is more conducive to discovering new ideas and receiving. It feels far more flexible and open than left-brain energy. It also feels much more feminine.

Moving from a linear, straight-path production mode to a winding path of exploration asks us to let go of agenda for a while. Instead of zeroing in on task completion, we are better served by focusing on serendipity. This energy has an ease about it that calls us to pay attention to what is. Observing all that is appearing around us, often at the exact right moment, we go after what sparks our attention. The discipline here is presence, not production. Are we able to stay in the current moment and notice the signs of guidance that are calling us forward?

As we cultivate our ability to be present, we will find that new avenues of inspiration appear in our lives with minimal prompting. And if we take time to set aside the structures we've built for our creative work, we may find that even a little bit of experimentation will allow for something completely new to emerge, simply because there are no restraints in place.

This experience of freedom might initially feel a bit daunting. But when we grant ourselves the gift of taking a creative side road, we get catapulted to places we would never have imagined previously. Places that leave us transformed in unexpected ways and lead us to new realms of possibility. Exploration quite naturally leads us to expansion. We may be surprised by what opens up as a result.

REFLECTIONS

- *How do you balance moving forward in a straight line with allowing a curving path of exploration in your creative work?*
- *What are some of the best ideas that have come to you when you've simply played and allowed your right brain full reign?*

24

INNER AUTHORITY

You already know the answers. They're within. Listen to
your voice, your spirit, your inner guidance.
It won't lead you astray.
—ELLE SOMMER

How well do you trust your inner authority? Most of our childhoods and teenage years are exercises in learning to listen to and trust external authorities—our parents, teachers, mentors, religious figures, and coaches. But at some point, we leave the nest and learn to fly on our own. Usually, this is signified by living independently. But we can live independently for decades and still not engage in the necessary work to fully trust our own inner compass. We can struggle with doubt, insecurity, and an inability to fully own our life choices, seeking stamps of validation to reassure us of our path.

However, we can also choose to use our experiences with outer authority to send us down a road that leads to an embracing of our own inner knowing. As we do, we stop trying to step into someone else's role and finally step into our own. Substantial spiritual growth happens when we make this shift.

Gary Zukav writes, "Spiritual growth requires the development of inner knowing and inner authority. It requires the heart, not the intellect." Indeed, the journey to embrace our inner authority requires us to know our heart well and to recognize it as a wellspring of both longing and truth.

You are gifted with an inner compass. A pilot light that knows your course *and* is committed to your development. Rest assured, your truth will never make you smaller. Quite the contrary, it will lead you into new realms of growth if you dare to listen and follow. Your own authority knows exactly what unexpressed reserves lie within. It is always calling you to awaken to new strengths.

My soul tells me what I want, and I'm living toward it with confidence. How well does this reflect your reality? And how well do you know the deposits in your own heart? Do you trust them? When we are repeatedly taught by systems, authorities, and gurus to look outside of ourselves for guidance, truth, reassurance, and knowledge, we risk overlooking the tremendous wealth that lies inside. And in many ways, we stay underdeveloped, lacking an internal strength and surety that knows precisely how to navigate and move toward our destinies.

Trusting our inner authority requires taking radical responsibility for our lives. To do this, we must own everything that belongs to us and recognize the power we carry to create our own realities. We take the responsibility to validate ourselves and affirm our own choices, no longer giving that task to someone else.

Ultimately, trusting our own authority means that we are willing to dare. We stop dismissing our ideas and begin to listen. We become willing to take risks, to trust inner nudges of guidance even when they are mere glimmers, and, no matter what unfolds, declare our lives worthy each step of the way. We are that powerful. The only thing hindering us is our belief.

REFLECTIONS

- *How well do you trust your inner knowing?*
- *In what ways has following your instincts led you to the next right thing?*
- *What outer authority do you need to come out from under?*

25

AMBITION

Tell me, what is it you plan to do with
your one wild and precious life?
—MARY OLIVER

I recently received an email whose subject line both drew me in and gave me pause. I wouldn't have flinched at it a few years ago. But after you move outside of the culture in which you were raised, you gain an ability to see it in a more discriminating and discerning light. Excesses that were not previously clear become more glaring.

Its subject line was: "How to Reach the 'Tipping Point' on Your Destiny Path & Manifest Something BIG in 9 Months by Becoming a Master Creator." This email came from an organization I admire. They offer a multitude of online educational opportunities related to self-actualization, discovering life purpose, and spirituality. I took one of their online courses a few years ago and had a very positive experience with it.

However, something about this subject line leaves me unsettled. It could be that I'm simply finding myself a bit more wary of anything feeling like propaganda these days. Or it could be that, because I have experienced so much abundance and true wealth living in Mexico, my heart is regularly full. Consequently, the constant American quest for "more, bigger, and faster" is starting to feel a bit perplexing. My current life experience is reinforcing the reality most of us already know—more, bigger, and faster are completely disconnected from soul fulfillment.

Now, when I see a subject line like the one above, I'm left asking, "Why do I need that?" This doesn't mean that I don't still have my own list of things to manifest. I have plenty of unmet goals and ambitions that I enjoy working toward. However, the line separating them from true satisfaction is more apparent here than in the States. While I am committed to living out my destiny path, I am becoming more detached from the results.

I think this different perspective stems, at least in part, from the fact that Mexican culture places a strong emphasis on experiencing life as a journey. In contrast, American culture is more focused on the destination, fixating on results and unachieved goals. But when you are fixated on what is not yet manifested, you are divorced from your present reality. Clearly, this subject line's wording and overall tone ask me to attach to outcome again. No matter how well-intentioned it might be, the bottom line is that it instructs my soul to stay in discontentment mode and attach to something not yet realized.

This contradicts the lessons I am currently learning. When you are encouraged to focus on the journey instead of obsessing over an unmet arrival, your soul benefits in some pretty amazing ways. You are still free to achieve, but your relationship with achieving feels qualitatively different. When you are immersed in a shared cultural recognition of what matters most in life, things like connection to others, a sense of purpose, meaningful work, and celebration, you are freed up to establish a healthier relationship with whatever outcomes you are moving toward. Restlessness takes a back seat to appreciation, and you become more grounded in the here and now.

Working toward success in whatever field you find yourself also becomes sustainable. It is woven into the fabric of life rather than being an imprint forced on top of everything else. Instead of being defined by workaholism and burnout, growth becomes regenerative, allowing for cycles.

Whether we desire to manifest our goals in two weeks, nine months, or next year, I think we would do well to question how our souls are faring in the midst of "more, bigger, and faster." Lightning-fast progress is not everything, after all. A little bit of discernment can help us recognize exactly what our souls are chasing and why.

REFLECTIONS

- *Where do you feel the pressure of "more, bigger, and faster" in your life?*

- *How can you give more weight to the journey of moving toward your goals and prioritize heart fulfillment along the way?*
- *What particular goals lead you to experience the most profound soul satisfaction?*

26

BEFRIENDING DOUBT

*The next time you realize doubts are part of your thought
process, revel in them—don't try to ignore them or set
them aside. Each doubt has a purpose, and if you
chew on them for a bit, they will show you the
way to the best possible decision. Being thoughtful
is a journey, and the journey never ends.*

—CONNIE CHWAN

Wavering is a decidedly normal part of a new venture.
On occasion, the genesis of an idea will come to us with
great clarity and certainty. But more frequently, ideas for
future steps arrive as slight impressions, faint ah-has, or
possible roads to take that are anything but concrete.

It takes time and exploration to fully embody a
new direction or sense of calling. And the journey to
get there can be filled with a lot of second-guessing.
But these moments of wavering don't necessarily signal
that we've made the wrong choice or are headed in the
wrong direction. They are a natural part of trying on
something new.

When in doubt, we may find ourselves looking
back fondly at what we've left behind, viewing the past
through rose-colored lenses. We might even forget

why we felt propelled to leave the old behind in the first place. We wonder if we've lost our way. But our instincts always serve a purpose, even with temporary lapses of forgetting. In the midst of uncertainty, our root impulses act as a homing pigeon, guiding us onward.

It serves us well to remember that doubts frequently surface when we intentionally explore uncharted territory or try something outside our comfort zone. They signify that a needed stretching is taking place. Therefore, the questioning we experience may, in fact, be a sign that we are on the cutting edge of our own growth. It is an affirmation in disguise of our own courage. Questions become a necessary part of walking out a process of embodiment, one in which we are internalizing profound shifts.

With this perspective, we can embrace our wavering without fear and trust that it will get resolved in its own time. We can choose to peacefully coexist with uncertainty, knowing that it won't remain forever. It is merely a temporary companion on the road to a newly created future.

REFLECTIONS

- *Are there ways in which you have let doubts derail you from a needed shift or change?*
- *Can you give ear to those doubts, and at the same time affirm the new ventures you are moving toward?*

27

THE BEAUTY OF CRACKS

Ring the bells that still can ring. Forget your perfect
offering. There is a crack in everything.
That's how the light gets in.
—LEONARD COHEN

I visited the Frida Kahlo Museum in Mexico City the other weekend. To be honest, I didn't know very much about Frida Kahlo before going. I was aware that she was a well-known Mexican artist married to Diego Rivera, but that was about the extent of my knowledge.

After seeing the neighborhood where she grew up and reading about her career and achievements, I came away impressed by her diligence and pursuit of her craft. Despite her many physical limitations and handicaps, she honored and honed her creative gifts. And she persevered despite her doubts, her lower status as a woman, and repeated questioning of her worth and the value of her work.

A light bulb went off in my head as I left the museum. Here Frida was, this shining example of living one's purpose and calling, *along with* all kinds of personal struggles and deficits. Her difficulties were not eradicated or swept under the rug. And she wasn't on a mission to fill in or fix all of these weaker, more vulnerable parts of her life experience. No, she simply managed to create with them all intact. And in fact, her art was very much informed by her physical disabilities, in particular. The imperfect parts of her life, or the "cracks," became an integral part of her life's work.

There is a Japanese art form that models this truth, the reality of our cracks becoming a vital part of the tapestry of our lives. Kintsugi, also known as kintsukuroi, uses a precious metal—liquid gold or silver—to bring together pieces of a broken pottery item and enhance the broken lines. In this way, the piece receives a new lease on life and becomes more refined, thanks to its scars. Kintsugi teaches that broken objects are not something to hide, but something to display with pride.

Maybe the goal isn't to fill in all of our cracks after all, despite what self-help culture tells us (not to mention that the quest to perfect our imperfections is a battle that's never won). Frida's life and work are inspiring and powerful precisely because of her limitations. They are what made her unique and gave her life distinctiveness. And the whole art form of kintsugi wouldn't exist without seeing the potential within broken pieces of clay. There is power in self-acceptance. Valuable energy is released when we stop obsessing over what is "not right" in ourselves and channel it toward our dreams instead.

Perhaps we can learn to see our own cracks in a new

light, and instead of our repeated attempts to eliminate them, choose to let them be filled with gold. As their appearance begins to change, may we begin to perceive them as a beautiful and integral part of all that we bring to the world.

REFLECTIONS

- *What are some ways you fall into the trap of constant self-improvement?*
- *How can you turn what you might consider a deficiency or weakness into a gift—a unique part of what you offer to others?*

28

DISMANTLING FEAR

Fear is the devil's greatest illusion.
—R.M. DRAKE

I recently went to teach at a university in Hong Kong. Before going, I read a CNN article on some of the restrictions the region is starting to face as China continues to exert greater levels of control. According to the author, the University of California school system had advised students and faculty traveling to Hong Kong not to use certain messaging apps, as communications are no longer private.

When I arrived, I asked my university professor friend if she had any concerns about China. I shared what I had read and asked what it felt like to live under the threat of communism. In turn, she surprised me with questions about gun control in the U.S. (or the lack thereof) and if I was ever worried about getting shot. This echoed a sentiment I've heard from several international friends recently who had been warned by advisories that many U.S. cities are not safe for travel. Before I moved to Mexico, many people in the U.S. expressed concern and inquired, "Is it safe?" and "Aren't you afraid of the cartels?" Their thinking was informed by a plethora of news reports warning of the drug trade.

These are just three of many examples that illustrate how frequently we are inundated with narratives of fear, especially when it comes to other places and people— even though people create safe and fulfilling lives in regions deemed "unsafe" all the time. Fearful messages are so ubiquitous, we're almost oblivious to them. But at the end of the day, *it is our perception of these messages that matters,* allowing our world to shrink or expand in response.

A narrative of fear springs from many places— certainly the media, but also what others tell us, or the mental chatter we tell ourselves about our own life experience. A good friend of mine recently began a romantic relationship with someone she has known for a long time. In telling me about this development, she said that she had resisted the possibility for years. But when she could finally identify that it was her fear holding her back, she was able to consciously overcome it and move forward with an exciting new chapter in her life.

Subconscious fears limit much of our life's movement. And no matter how they arise—whether from an external source or an internal hesitation—they will always serve to keep our worlds restricted, having a diminishing effect on our souls. Fear keeps us from living the fullest lives of which we are capable.

We support our own growth, therefore, every time we examine the relationship between fear and our beliefs. We are frequently taught that "the other" (person, place, or life experience) is something to mistrust. And to compound matters, what is familiar to us is always what will feel safest, whether this is actually true or not. It will help us, then, to remember that fear creates only an *illusion* of safety. Although seductive, it results in a sense of separateness from the world around us and our fellow humans.

Most likely, we will need to challenge a narrative (or two) that we've decided is true and, instead, explore the possibility of a different reality. In the process, we may find ourselves liberated from various restrictions we've erected, discovering that the particular script we've believed is not as accurate as we once thought.

The work of dismantling fear in our lives, although not easy, is fruitful. In doing it, we make a habit of regularly challenging our own thinking and consciously open up to a broader realm of possibility (whose potentialities may surprise us!). At the end of each day, how we perceive the world will determine where we allow life to take us.

REFLECTIONS

- *Where have you been shrinking from fear as of late?*
- *Are there obvious or subtle ways your life has been made smaller because of a narrative of fear?*
- *What is one step you can take today to start*

*challenging your perceptions and rise above what
your fear claims as truth?*

29

GRANTING OURSELVES FREEDOM

You find freedom inside—nowhere else. In the heart of
every human being is that one space which is free.
—PREM RAWAT

Remembering that freedom is an inside job will serve us well on our creative journey. Too often we forget this, expecting that it comes from someone or something outside of us—another person's permission or approval, an opportunity granted to us, or an understanding of our chosen path.

But in looking to someone or something else to give what we are fully capable of granting ourselves, we give away our power. We think, *If she would just be willing to offer her support…* or *If he would show interest in the goals I'm working toward…* or *If that career door would open, then my inner artist could really soar!* We create conditions that limit our movement. But it is misguided to wait for something in the external world to shift before we set forth and start developing our gifts. Transformation only ever starts by changing things inside ourselves first—our own thinking, our beliefs, and the actions that flow from them. Every moment of every day, we have the power to shift what we believe and how much freedom we choose to embrace.

For a long time, I experienced all kinds of self-imposed limitations because someone I was close to didn't see the value in my creative work. This was hurtful, and at times made me question myself. I had to remind myself repeatedly over the years that I didn't need to be bound by these limited views because *they were her limited views,* not mine.

Instead of waiting for others to change, or to realize that creative work is as important as any other kind of work, I needed to believe it myself. We have the power to choose to value our creative gifts, no matter who offers a stamp of approval or what career doors do or do not open. When we remember that we have that power, we suddenly feel less constricted inside. We start to operate from a renewed place of strength instead of self-doubt. Our sense of what is possible begins to expand. And suddenly, things that felt like obstacles diminish or disappear entirely.

It can take time to extract ourselves from the opinions and views of those around us. But the liberating truth we must always return to is that we are not dependent on others to reflect what we need. We can give ourselves what we need, as often as we need it. We liberate our own souls.

REFLECTIONS

- *Where have you felt stuck or limited because you were waiting for another person or an external circumstance to change?*
- *What is one way you can grant yourself the freedom and permission you need to move forward with your creative work?*

30
EXPANSION DISGUISED

To fully live is to engage in a continual pattern of release and forward motion. We let go of old forms of manifesting in order to make way for new ones that are asking to be birthed. These new forms do not come to us fully defined or fully seen. They come to us shrouded in mystery, with just enough showing that we are captivated and willing to leap forward into the unknown to seek out their shimmering newness.

Our path becomes hindered if we allow the old to attach as baggage that we drag behind. It is with both trepidation and excitement that we cut those cords and release. We step into a yet unshaped future, one that allows for a greater emergence after a time of fertile work.

—JOURNAL ENTRY, FEBRUARY 10, 2016

Expansion brings excitement, the promise of something new, and, indeed, something "shimmering"—as I wrote in my journal the year I was moving from an art career to that of a writer. Expansion brings a sense of possibility and encourages us to mine areas of our lives and gifts that are untapped.

Despite the excitement that expansion can bring, it doesn't always appear in our lives as a sparkly, shiny new package to be opened. Sometimes it arrives at our doorstep looking quite the opposite—dressed in the guise of change, staleness, or loss. A job that has run its course. A missed opportunity. A withering relationship. Or, it may simply be the awareness that we've outgrown old ways of being and doing.

But what might appear on the surface as something gone stale or a dead-end staring us in the face is, in actuality, the creation of space and fertile ground for something new. When what we thought was a guaranteed opportunity or direction falls away, or when familiar ways of existing in the world suddenly stop working, we have the opportunity to expand. And in the process, we may find ourselves aligning even more with who we really are.

An artist friend of mine recently went through a period of extreme shifts and disappointments in her life, losing both her physical health and a job that she loved as a result. Her recovery was long and arduous, and many times along the way she lost hope. But, as she persisted in making her way through the grieving and eventual healing process, she told me that the life changes she experienced were converted into "God incubators," or spaces where the Divine came to dwell, heal her pain, and plant new seeds and dreams—ones that felt even more in tune with what she really wanted to do. She told me that each day became an opportunity to receive these shifts as a gift. Instead of resisting them, or worse, giving in to a victim mentality and wallowing in self-pity, she chose to experience them as the ground upon which a brighter vision for her future could begin to emerge. She began to trust, as much as she was able, that expansion was on its way.

The writer Henry Thoreau, before settling down by Walden Pond, spent a year living in New York City and pursuing its literary scene. He went to the big city to find writing success in the conventional way. While there, almost all of his work was rejected by the well-known writers and publishers of his day. But it was these disappointments that propelled him to return to his cabin in the woods and live the mystic life that called to him, writing what eventually became his greatest and most famous works. What looked like a dead end in New York resulted in a truly destined career expansion that he could never have previously imagined.

We must pay close attention to the less-than-ideal circumstances in our lives. Oftentimes they are gifts of expansion in disguise. Feelings of staleness or unasked-for life shifts may actually be signposts asking us to explore a new direction or release something that no longer works. Sometimes growth looks like contraction at first. But if we look carefully, *shimmering newness* is hiding beneath the surface. And with it comes new energy. May we have the courage to nurture these seeds of possibility into beautiful fruit.

REFLECTIONS

- *Have you recently experienced unexpected change or disappointment? If so, what kinds of new things can you imagine growing in the space the disappointment has left behind?*
- *Is there something you need to let go of to allow a new direction to take root?*

31

THE VALUE OF A FULL HEART

Your life is only as full as your heart.
—PEPI NAKI

Does fullness count? This is the question dancing around in my mind today as I soak in my surroundings, watching the trees sway in the wind from the outdoor table where I sit and reflect. An inner sense of fullness and contentment is a state of being I have come to experience regularly in Mexico. However, I admit I am more used to running on empty, whether work-wise, relationship-wise, or just plain effort-wise. I come from a culture that encourages wearing exhaustion and over-busyness as badges of merit on your sleeve.

It is from this cultural narrative that I ask myself, "Is a state of fullness even allowed?" And beyond that, is it possibly a hallmark of "enough"? I wonder this as I struggle with doubts and a lack of clarity regarding my future steps, not quite sure of this unfamiliar path unfolding before me.

I would imagine that many in the United States are familiar with the cultural preference for running on empty. Meaningful activity and heart satisfaction are usurped by productivity and making money, and we often ignore what is in the depth of our soul. There is frequently little time for the things that truly fill us up, such as relaxing with friends and family, celebrations of life events, and a shared sense of camaraderie with those around us.

However, output is not sustainable when it is just one-way, and running on empty is not a gauge of true success. A full heart is a vital indicator of our well-being. And it is only when we allow a sense of replenishment into our lives that we are empowered to operate from a healthy and strong center.

As I watch the limbs of the trees rock back and forth in the gentle breeze, I intuitively sense that a similar breeze is stirring desires in my heart. Stagnant air is being pushed away. And, in the midst of asking *"Is this fullness allowed?"* as if to somehow assuage the guilt I feel at this state of wholeness, I realize that I am at the beginning of learning how to follow this fresh wind. There are tastes and glimpses of it everywhere.

And so, the choice is mine. Instead of running on empty, I will practice choosing what fills me up. I am finding this new way of being too life-giving to ignore.

REFLECTIONS

- *Is it easier for you to give more value to over-busyness and exhaustion than to filling your own cup?*

- *What activities, people, or places refill your heart?*
  Choose one replenishing thing you can do this week.

32

GROWING STILL

Only in quiet waters do things mirror themselves undistorted. Only in a quiet mind is an adequate perception of the world.
—HANS MARGOLIUS

I've been struggling with insomnia lately. Maybe this is just a sign of middle age. My high school friend Jennifer regularly finds herself up in the middle of the night, and we joke about middle age becoming the new old age. As a single mom, her life is full of young children, full-time work, and a never-ending to-do list. She feels the brunt of busyness more than most. But we have concluded that in lives lived to the hilt, with constant demands on one's time and attention, these unasked-for bouts of sleeplessness offer one very important gift: the gift of stillness.

Stillness is virtually an extinct commodity in this day and age. Few people create lives that allow for it, and fewer still actually choose it when it presents itself. But while these quiet periods may arise at inopportune times, like a restless awakening in the middle of the night, we always have the choice to see stillness for what it truly is—a portal to something sacred.

Cultural trends support this truth. Is it any wonder that things like meditation, yoga, and silent retreats have gained such traction in our society? People crave moments of solitude and are even willing to pay to make them happen. This is a testament to the transformative beauty of slowing down our lives to simply be.

What is it that transpires in these moments? What makes them so beautiful? For one, stillness is when perspective begins to flood in—it allows us to hear the voice of Spirit. We start to see signs of guidance that we overlooked in all our busyness. We receive intuitive direction for our next steps. Our souls become nourished and our minds stop chattering. We lay down burdens and release our worries. We breathe more deeply, and our emotions calm down. Or perhaps they get more intense as we finally let them out. Being still is a release. We feel support from God, the Universe, and our higher knowing, becoming more oriented to the *real* reality. We come away centered and grounded.

It is easy to lose our way in the midst of life's commotion. But when we do, may we seek out these rare and precious moments of stillness. May we allow them to happen. In creating a gateway for peace to enter, we will find ourselves again.

REFLECTIONS

- *Find ten minutes a day where you can become still and simply be with whatever arises.*
- *Finish this sentence: "When I grow still. . ."*

33

EMBRACING "ENOUGH"

It's a funny thing about life, once you begin to take note of the things you are grateful for, you begin to lose sight of the things that you lack.

—GERMANY KENT

"There is a way that we keep moving in our culture that really doesn't help us get ahead." I wrote down this sentiment years ago and have never quite forgotten it, as it sums up a tremendous amount of truth in just one sentence. It describes so well what I feel in American culture daily...a need for constant movement and an internal striving that rarely seems to produce something fruitful.

What is this about? You could describe it in many ways. It could be defined as a need for continuous improvement or a never-ending quest to get what is still out of reach. Or possibly a perpetual but often hidden dissatisfaction with what is. A nagging feeling that somehow, what I have or who I am or what I do is not yet enough.

This concept of being enough runs deep. A simple look at advertising alone confirms this. Almost every billboard, Internet, TV, or radio ad bases at least part of its message on the need for something to be bought, changed, improved, or fixed. Just how much of what drives us in life is this ubiquitous mandate to upgrade our lives, buoyed by an underlying fear of not measuring up? A conviction that somehow, we are not yet what we should be. Subscribing to a belief in deficiency creates a tremendous amount of false pressure in our lives. It keeps us on the treadmill of our choice. And it erodes our quality of life and the experience of joy.

Some of the happiest people I've ever encountered have either lived in or come from countries where people generally have less and are more able to "be" in the midst of whatever life is currently offering. They are not as preoccupied with the quest for *more* that permeates American culture, perhaps seeing it clearly for what it is: an illusion that never quite delivers what it promises.

It is our thinking that needs to change, much more than our circumstances themselves. Maybe who we are and the inevitable mix of ups and downs that accompanies our lives is a mirror of plenitude we have failed to recognize. If so, we can exchange some of our need to strive and constantly be in motion for greater internal freedom instead.

Contrary to what some may think, embracing the idea of "enough" doesn't equal passivity or indicate that you've ceased moving forward in life. It simply means that you've decided to walk in a spirit of gratitude and experience satisfaction with things *as they are*, in this moment. And it embodies an instinctive knowing that we, ourselves, are enough, just as we are. The gift of liberation we will receive in return is far more valuable than what any pursuit of "more" may promise.

REFLECTIONS

- *In what ways have you internalized society's messages of not being, doing, or having enough?*
- *How can you intentionally prioritize contentment and gratitude over the need to constantly chase something out of reach?*

34

INTERDEPENDENCE

Only by giving are you able to receive
more than you already have.
—JIM ROHN

She sits on the corner, an elderly woman with a colorful scarf wrapped around her hair. Her wizened face peeks out from beneath it, and her dim eyes glance hesitantly upward at the strangers passing by. She extends her gnarled hand, patiently awaiting any offering. Most ignore her presence, but soon, a middle-aged man drops a few coins in her palm and continues on.

I am on my way to buy coffee, something I do many days when I am out and about. It's one of life's small pleasures, and given that a cup of coffee here is about half the cost of what it is in Los Angeles, I am feeling a bit of extra freedom to indulge. I pass by the woman on the corner and think about her as I stand in line a block away to purchase my drink.

In every city I've ever lived in, I've often passed people on the street asking for money. So it's a familiar sight. But today, something about this particular woman speaks to me. I can't quite put my finger on what it is.

In my spirit, I feel the need to give her a gift. After getting my coffee, I turn to walk in her direction and, as I approach, bend down to drop a bill in her hand. She grasps it loosely, and it falls to the sidewalk. I reach down to retrieve it and hand it to her again, smiling and saying "Dios le bendiga" or "God bless you." Her face lights up, and her eyes begin to shine.

Something about this interaction touches me. I realize anew that I need what she imparts to me in her response, just as much as she needs financial help. For giving does something vital for our souls. Small or large, any gift to a fellow human being deposits something profound in our spirits. Our hearts both soften and enlarge, and we discover that the essence of the exchange pours grace and love into our very being.

I walk away thinking about her, filled with both an appreciation for our interconnectedness and a more in-depth understanding of our interdependence. I am filled with gratitude, both for her need and for an awareness of my own. Together, we serve one another.

REFLECTIONS

- *How has an experience of giving to others moved you in unexpected ways?*
- *What has it taught you about your interdependence with those around you?*

35

PERSISTENCE

What if you didn't take the process and the results
personally? What if you just got busy with the next
possibility and the next? A dandelion doesn't cast a seed
and then hold its breath and wait to see if and how it
takes root. It keeps casting seeds. It gives everything it has
to everything it is born to do. What if you kept casting
your seeds to the wind—and it didn't matter which seed
took root because you knew something would. That's the
nature of creation. Something always comes through.

—TAMA KIEVES

Persist we must, if our art is to ever make its debut into the world. I am part of a weekly writers' group, and on any given week between five and ten people gather, computers in tow. All who come desire to give birth to their writing creations, contribute to the public sphere, and offer something of hope, challenge, or thoughtfulness to society.

But these offerings don't come about merely through wishful thinking or by showing up occasionally to write a few lines. No, the name of the game with any creative endeavor is dogged persistence. In fact, one of the group members, a woman named Lainey, persevered mightily in writing her first novel. Upon completion, she sent it to countless agents, all of whom rejected it. Two years later, and after 130 rejections, her work was finally accepted by a small publishing company. Just when she was about to give up hope and accept that this particular work would never see the light of day, publishing became a tangible option. But if it weren't for that last bit of tenacity, her work may have remained unexpressed to the larger world.

Anyone who thinks the creative life is somehow easy or a glorified path of self-expression would do well to remember that creative birthing is much more about the difficult work of staying the course than it is about being divinely inspired. It is about persisting when you are riding high on inspiration and when you are plagued with doubts, when the world doesn't believe in you, or when you fail to believe in yourself. Returning to our craft day after day, week after week, and consciously choosing to believe in our vision, even when it's cloudy, is the only way to transform ideas into something tangible.

The good news is, the ability to stick with our craft is a skill we can choose to cultivate, a muscle that grows stronger each time we use it. By staying the course, we take a stand in owning our power and affirming that our creations want and need to be shared with others. Determination forms habits and habits lead to finished work. And finished work will always find its place in the world if we fail to give up.

REFLECTIONS

- *What specific discipline helps move your creative work forward?*
- *Where can you receive support from other creatives to help you push through adversity and stick with your craft?*

36

LISTENING TO YOUR INNER CHILD

*Being an artist is a dream that is championed and
protected by your inner child. Our inner child
is the innocent, fun, and playful spirit that
believes it can do and be anything.*

—COLBY RICE

Our creativity is very much like a small child. And often, it helps when we talk to it that way, asking questions like, "How are you feeling today?" "What do you need?" And "How can I help you feel safe and supported?"

I'm writing this while sitting in a quiet and peaceful park near my home. My inner artist knew she needed the beauty of the trees today. In fact, she asked for it. And I'm glad that I listened and didn't brush her off like we so easily do with small children. "Not now," we say, giving in to the belief that other things are more important than a child's momentary wishes.

Over the years, I have learned that my inner artist needs a regular connection to nature in order to thrive. And it is in my creativity's best interest to listen and provide these environments as often as possible. In these settings ideas begin to flow, I more easily hear solutions to creative problems, and I get glimpses of future projects waiting to be born.

Today, I am feeling grateful that I paid attention to my inner artist and didn't rush ahead with my adult self, believing the common sentiment that our creativity is always for "another time." It is easy to discount our creative children, isn't it? They don't demand our attention the way other people or tasks do. They don't walk around with an air of their own self-importance.

But maybe it is because of their unassuming nature that they are precisely the voices we need to be listening to more often. Their insights might surprise us and shake us out of our routine. When you feel blocked, your inner creative child just might know a way forward. She is always chock full of ingenuity and cleverness.

The next time your creative spirit taps you on the shoulder, take a moment to slow down and listen. Become a receptive partner and practice honoring her requests. You never know what fresh inspiration will follow.

REFLECTIONS

- *What are some of the wishes of your inner creative child?*
- *What are some ways you can give energy and attention to those wishes this week?*

37

LIVING INTO LARGENESS

*Never underestimate the power of dreams and the
influence of the human spirit. We are all the
same in this notion: The potential for
greatness lives within each of us.*
—WILMA RUDOLPH

Imagine a world where you feel no limits, external or
internal. What inside you would expand? What would
come to the forefront to be expressed? Is there a hidden
longing within you yearning to find its place in the
world? We each have greater capacities within us, calling
to be birthed in this particular time and place. James
Hollis writes, "And yet each of us has an appointment
with ourselves, with our own soul."

New York Times bestselling author Sue Monk Kidd
calls these capacities within each of us "the stamp of
our unique genius." She explores this concept through
her female protagonist, a young woman named Ana, in
The Book of Longings. Ana is on a quest to live out the
largeness she senses within herself, all of her unexpressed
capabilities. She faces numerous obstacles—from her
family, the time period she was born, and her own

inner struggles. But amid a myriad of challenges, she is emboldened by both her aunt's belief in her greatness and her growing confidence that she is meant for more than what her culture expects of her.

We have a choice as to whether or not we will step into the possibility of a larger life. But, as James Hollis writes, "Whether we keep that appointment and step into the largeness of the summons is another matter." Although the journey to overcome both real and perceived limits is never obstacle-free, one way we begin to live out our untapped potential is by forming alliances with others who can accompany us on the journey, calling out our abilities when we cannot see them ourselves. In turn, we call out theirs, and a beautiful exchange is born. At its core, enlarging is relational, and we have a responsibility to one another's transformation. Mirroring relationships that call forth our greatest gifts illuminate for us what it means to partner with one another. We learn to bear witness to one another's light.

Likewise, there are seasons in life when we must take it upon ourselves to bless our own largeness. We may not always have an advocate in our corner cheering us on. And in those times, we must choose to believe in ourselves, mightily. Cultivating our own journey of empowerment is a vital building block for our own rising. Each day, we have the ability to nurture and affirm in ourselves what we dream of being.

Growing in self-empowerment and choosing to partner with others are powerful forces. Held together in balance, these twin energies get activated. The act of blessing our inherent largeness—on our own accord and together with like-minded souls—will never fail to set our souls on fire.

REFLECTIONS

- *Is there a hidden longing within you yearning to find its place in the world?*
- *With whom can you cultivate a mirroring relationship, each calling forth one another's untapped potential?*

38

SOARING

*Stop strategizing and start listening. Trust that
life is indeed organizing around your success.*
—CLAIRE ZAMMIT

Soaring weight-free. My friend calls from New Mexico this morning, telling me these words are the invitation before her this week. She is promoting her newly released book and feels pressure to make it a big splash in the world. She is caught in a web of strategizing, attempting to predict outcomes with calculations based on other writers' methods, and her inner critic is telling her that her marketing efforts aren't enough. Feeling frustrated and in need of a break, she stepped outside to take in the wide expanse of nature beckoning to her through her window.

As she glanced at the sky above, a majestic eagle soared past, wings spread wide, floating amidst the clouds. Its beauty was stunning. The currents of the wind supported its flight and modeled a call, a faint whisper of guidance.... *Soaring is an invitation for today, a path forward out of the web that has you stuck. A new way to engage with life.* This is the gift being deposited into my friend's heart this week as she promotes her book: an experience of being supported by the currents of the wind. It is a compelling suggestion, and an attractive way to partner with her creative desires and the work she feels called to do.

But what, exactly, does this mean? Oftentimes our best attempts at strategy end up being a heavy load that leaves us limited in choice and movement. And our comparisons to others keep us stuck. Efforts to wrangle our lives and work inadvertently become more about striving and copying someone else's version of success. Somewhere along the way, we end up trading expansive thought for restricted thinking, feeling the weight of our destinies upon our shoulders.

In contrast, the eagle's flight mirrors a different reality, one in which we *follow and respond to life-giving energy, not pressure.* Soaring embodies the ability to receive, allow, and partner with the essence of life around us. These words alone carry a freedom that "strategizing" does not. And they include following our own unique creative path and not trying to live someone else's. This speaks to my friend as she considers the eagle's invitation to an experience of weightless flight. This is the permission she needs to unload her burdens and fruitless attempts at comparison. She can finally release the pressure she's been carrying and allow her empty reservoirs to be filled.

As we move beyond the scope of our box-like expectations and begin to let our intuition guide, we become free to soar and create unhindered, in ways that truly match our innermost selves. Instead of feeling burdened by narrow outcomes, we open to a wider sea of possibility. And we are liberated to embrace a way of moving in the world that truly nourishes our souls.

REFLECTIONS

- *Has overly strategizing about particular challenges left you feeling stuck?*
- *What expectations of your work have become burdens that need to be released?*
- *Pay attention to what feels most life-giving to you. In what ways can you listen to these signs of life and to your core essence? They are the cues that will best support your creative flight.*

39

THE GIFT OF WAITING

The primary cause of unhappiness is never the situation but your thoughts about it.
—ECKHART TOLLE

To be in a hurry in Mexico is to miss the point. I am writing this not from theory but from practice, as I sit here waiting for a taxi at the botanical gardens just outside of town. Mexico operates with a very different sense of time than its northern neighbor. In the States, most things are presented as urgent. And even things that truly aren't urgent are often perceived as nuisances to rush through.

However, this is not true in Mexico. Patience, coupled with an innate ability to just *be* in the present moment, is embedded in the culture. It is something I am quite envious of, actually. Because if I observe when I grow impatient, it is rarely because I genuinely need something faster. It is primarily because I have a cultural urge within me to speed everything up. And if I really examine this urge, it becomes clear that instead of serving me in some capacity, it only ends up controlling me.

The botanical gardens are located in a remote part of town and since few cars pass by, the staff regularly call taxis to pick up waiting passengers. As I sit by the exit, I overhear a group of Americans in line ahead of me sharing their frustration. They have been waiting for twenty minutes for their cab, and a few other taxis have dropped people off in the meantime. However, you are supposed to wait for the car that was called for you and not leave in a different one before it arrives. Otherwise, the driver will have made a wasted trip.

The Americans ahead of me have chosen to wait for their en route taxi but are now regretting it, wishing they had jumped in the last one that pulled away. Their cultural preference for efficiency is starting to take over and detract from what has been a relaxing afternoon in a tranquil setting.

Waiting for a taxi in Mexico is but one example of the myriad of ways life offers us opportunities to resist our own entrenched sense of hurry. When we do so, we discover that these unasked-for times of waiting are actually mini-exercises in practicing freedom. Impatience will try to control us and rob us of our ability to be in the present moment. But when forced to wait, we are given the gift of fully entering our current reality and are liberated from a sense of time that fills our thinking with unnecessary restraints. Space opens up in our hearts, creating room for greater awareness and appreciation for what lies in front of us.

REFLECTIONS

- *When you hurry, how does it fuel your own sense of dissatisfaction?*
- *How can you turn periods of waiting into opportunities for greater self-awareness and appreciation for the present?*

40

THE UPSIDE OF PROCRASTINATION

If you find a path with no obstacles,
it probably doesn't lead anywhere.
—FRANK A. CLARK

Not all procrastination is a bad thing, contrary to popular belief. In fact, our times of procrastination can actually be a sign that we're on the right path. As Steven Pressfield suggests in *The War of Art,* the resistance we often encounter along our creative path is directly tied to our soul's own evolution. Meaning, the more our creative work aligns with what we are meant to do and be in the world, the more resistance we will feel in pursuing it. Hence, procrastination.

I know this reality very well. One of my goals for this year has been to transfer my partially written book from a myriad of text edit files into the Scrivener writing app. I used Scrivener for my first book and found it quite helpful, but I haven't used it for three years. So my brain needs a refresher on the mechanics of how it works.

I've been avoiding reacquainting myself with the software for over a week now, and thinking this is because I dislike technology. But today, after finally making myself sit down to transfer the entire content, I realize that my dislike of technology is masking an underlying reality—*producing another book scares me.*

Why? Because I know deep down that writing and producing more books is exactly what I am supposed to be doing in the world. And to do so requires vulnerability. And traversing outside of my comfort zone. And being willing to embrace a greater degree of visibility. But it is work that is inextricably tied to my soul's next evolution—to my own transformation. And although I've been on a writing path for a long time now, it doesn't necessarily make it any easier. When we are committed to pushing the envelope of what we are called to be in the world, experiencing resistance is going to be par for the course.

Remember to take heart the next time you find yourself procrastinating with your creative work. It might just be that the very thing you're avoiding is *exactly* what you're meant to be giving to the world. Use signs of procrastination as a confirmation to gently push yourself over your avoidance hump and on your way. After all, your untapped potential won't do any good remaining unexpressed. The world needs what you have to offer, and so do you.

REFLECTIONS

- *What have you been avoiding lately?*

- *How can you use feelings of resistance as a motivator and potential affirmation that you are on the right path?*

41

LEARNING TO RECEIVE

*Until we can receive with an open heart, we're never
really giving with an open heart. When we attach
judgment to receiving help, we knowingly or
unknowingly attach judgment to giving help.*
—BRENÉ BROWN

Life will give us many opportunities to learn to receive
from others, if we are willing students. As a foreigner
living in another country, there is a fair amount I don't
know or understand, and I frequently need to ask those
around me for help.

Fortunately, Mexico is an extremely service-oriented
society, and assisting others is the norm. But it took
some time to relinquish my "do it yourself" American
tendencies, and my efforts to embrace a more receiving
mindset are still a work in progress. Changing the brain
pattern that places the burden of living on my own
shoulders to one shared amongst many shoulders requires
a complete rewiring. But it is a rewiring I am welcoming.

The daily gift of receiving help from those around
me has altered my soul in profound ways. It has made
me question the worship of self-sufficiency in my own

country. It has changed my beliefs about what real strength is. And now, instead of believing that doing things independently is of higher value, I see clearly that our real value is found in one another.

When I first landed in Mexico, I was taken aback by the airplane pilot who offered to put my cumbersome suitcases through the security conveyor belt himself. He had flown my plane and we were exiting the airport at the same time. My first inclination was to politely decline his help. However, I quickly thought better of it and proceeded to accept his assistance.

But declining is what we do when we've been conditioned to believe that doing things ourselves is the preferable choice. A gift is put on our plate (and may, in fact, be staring us in the face), and although the logical and most beneficial response would be to say "yes," we end up saying "no." We fail to recognize that the gift is ours to receive. The challenge is to give ourselves permission.

What is it that gets in the way of receiving help from others? Saying "yes" is difficult when we believe we don't deserve the assistance being offered to us in the moment. We think we must "work hard" for it because help must be earned, after all. What appears to be a free gift must have strings attached. Or maybe we fear that if we take too much from others, we will become a burden to them. And so, to protect others from carrying our weight, we decline. But regardless of what belief we allow to limit us, if our thinking remains unexamined, it will keep us from experiencing the meaning of true partnership with others.

We find sustenance in the practice of receiving from one another. We relinquish the myth that strength comes by doing life on our own, and we open to the truth that our greatest strength is found together and in each other. As we accept support, we release others to experience the gift of offering it. And this interchange—receiving, giving, and then receiving again—becomes a beautiful dance that reminds us of our interconnectedness and of our humanity.

REFLECTIONS

- *How easy is it for you to receive from others?*
- *Do you suffer from a lone ranger mindset that keeps you from the riches of connection and support?*
- *Ask yourself the question: "In what ways do I need to begin to receive?"*

42

EXERTING QUIET INFLUENCE

The secret to life is to put yourself in the right lighting. For some, it's a Broadway spotlight; for others, a lamplit desk.
—SUSAN CAIN

We live in a world where exciting fanfare and loud voices get the most attention. What does this mean for the creative soul who is most at home in the studio? So many artists and writers I know fit in this category, as creating necessitates copious amounts of time spent by oneself. An artist friend in LA told me that he hates going to art shows (despite needing to exhibit his own work). He describes galleries as rooms full of preening people, there to see and be seen: "The epitome of a tasteless display," he said. He will go to his friends' art shows to support their work, but that is his limit.

I know the feeling. I am most happy and content when writing or creating in my studio. And going public with my work is primarily tied to career opportunities, instead of an interest in being a focal point for others. Although there are many effective ways to market one's work, it is hard to escape the American preference for big, loud, and eye-catching. We celebrate the demonstrative. We are lured by what is flashy.

This ubiquitous cultural preference is part of what made Susan Cain's book *Quiet* so profound. In it, she sets the stage for elevating the unique way that those who are quieter by nature influence others. She describes these kinds of people as ones who "innovate and create, but dislike self-promotion, who favor working on their own over working in teams." She writes, "It is to introverts, such as Rosa Parks, Chopin, Dr. Seuss, Steve Wozniak—that we owe many of the great contributions to society."

And indeed, there are numerous alternative ways to create impact in an overly noisy world. Influence does not have to arrive in a supersized package. In fact, some of the best ways to persist on a creative path are tied to less flashy, but just as important ways of being and doing—things like persistence, thinking outside of the box, concentration, and observing and making commentary on what others miss.

I have contemplated this path of quiet influencing a lot throughout my creative career, and have found that the work of being a writer is in some ways even quieter in nature than that of an artist. There is not as much fanfare or showing of work in the same manner, with large crowds and socializing. But writing is undoubtedly just as potent an expression, and can pierce the heart with truth. Writers may never know just how widely their work is read, but their willingness to engage in this solitary pursuit can make a significant cultural impact.

An interior designer friend of mine has found great success in building one-on-one relationships with clients, something that comes very easily to most introverts. She runs her creative business with a partner, and it is my friend's job to maintain the company's Instagram page. And while she sometimes feels pressure to constantly post and build a sizable (read *huge*) follower count, nothing about that goal motivates or drives her. Instead of mass broadcasting, her persistence in making these quieter networking efforts over the long haul have paid off, resulting in a very successful business.

If you too find yourself in the camp of quieter creatives, don't be afraid to take a divergent approach with your work. Trust the way you are called to influence, even if it doesn't fit prevailing cultural norms. Your work will speak volumes in its own way.

REFLECTIONS

- *What is your preferred way to share your work with the world?*
- *Have you tried to conform to others' standards of influencing that don't fit your true nature?*
- *What ways of expressing yourself feel most authentically you and have the most impact?*

43

STEPPING COURAGEOUSLY INTO OUR PRESENT

*If you keep looking behind, you'll
miss the blessings in front of you.*
—ANONYMOUS

An old friend's news stirs something in me. First, it is a passing wave of envy. And then it morphs into feelings of doubt, leading me to wonder if I've made the right decision to begin this new chapter of my life as a writer and teacher in Mexico. My friend is a very talented musician based in the States, and recently some amazing career opportunities opened for him.

His news leads me to think about my time as an artist in Los Angeles. LA truly is the land of opportunity for creatives of all stripes. Many career doors opened for me during my time living there. And though I made a very conscious and clear choice to move on from that season for many compelling reasons, my friend's announcement has me looking back on LA with a bit of longing again. It deposits within me a seed of uncertainty regarding my new path.

I go upstairs to our roof deck to clean up debris from

a wind storm the night before. The wind has knocked over a pot, and it's broken into several pieces. The plant, however, has not suffered any damage. It has all kinds of new growth on it, including some fresh flowers that are blooming. My landlady suggests we replant it in the downstairs garden.

As I begin digging a hole for the container-less plant, I have an ah-ha moment in my spirit. Greater clarity regarding my morning thoughts comes seeping in. Fixating on my previous season in LA is the same as choosing to place my focus on the cracked pot in front of me. Over a year ago, I wrote in my journal that Los Angeles had become too small a container for what was to be birthed in me next. The evolution of my life had simply outgrown it, and I knew that I needed to be planted in new soil.

Like the plant I now hold in my hands, flowering with new shoots, all kinds of growth is beginning to emerge from my life. And the truth is, I *know* I am flourishing on my new trajectory. If I am honest, my life is thriving and many good things are happening. And I had needed a new container to bring about this joyful expansion.

The new shoots are where my focus needs to be, not on the cracked pot of an old season. I need to refocus my mind on the thriving around me and immerse myself in the beauty of the present moment. For everything has and is playing its role. With this new lens, I can now celebrate my friend's succe*ss and not let his path make me* *doubt my own.*

How often do we trade our present reality for dreams of the past, looking longingly at a time gone by instead of embracing the new ground upon which we stand? It is human nature to reminisce, but envying something we have left behind keeps us from stepping courageously into our present. It keeps us stuck in uncertainty, buffeted by doubts.

When we summon the strength to release our ties to the past and stand in solidarity with our soul's own growth, we are led to exactly where we need to be. We can trust the ground in which we are planted and allow it to do its work.

REFLECTIONS

- *Think of a time when you allowed thoughts of the past to cast doubt on your present life's journey. How did you overcome your uncertainty?*
- *How is your current environment supporting the growth you are called to in this season of life?*

44

PERSONAL POWER

When we get comfortable with our own strength,
discomfort changes shape. We remember our power.
—JEN KNOX

Recently I found out that my mom's health is in steep decline. The news came as a shock. She has lived with Parkinson's for over a decade, but thus far, it has been a very slow, degenerative disease. Now, seemingly overnight, serious dementia has set in, along with severe physical decline.

My first response is to sink into despair, fearing this means she is close to death. Indeed, hospice care is called in, and the nurses estimate she may only have six months left. My biggest anxiety is how to visit her, as the care facility she has been admitted to has strict COVID rules and quarantine restrictions for all guests. I begin to feel that life is happening *to me* instead of *for me,* and can feel myself collapsing under the weight of it all.

Days later, still in sadness and confusion, a small ray of light penetrates my outlook. It comes via a phone call with a dear friend. She helps me get in touch with my intentions, which are twofold—to hug my mom, despite the social distancing restrictions in place that do not allow physical contact, and to impart words of love and goodbye while a piece of her still knows who I am. I'm not exactly sure how these things will happen, given the strictness with which COVID rules are enforced. But my friend reminds me of the precious truth that my own personal power is still intact and that I need to use it to set my desires in motion.

Invigorated by this new perspective, I immediately change my flight to depart in two days, knowing that in order to achieve my desire, the sooner I arrive the better. Swimming in my anxiety at home won't serve anyone. This small but significant action is the beginning of me reclaiming my power in what otherwise feels like a hopeless situation.

Days after this personal shift, my father decides to remove my mom from the isolation of the care facility and bring her back home, hiring round-the-clock caregivers. Although this is not a financially sustainable option long-term, the choice allows us to fully say our goodbyes. A wave of relief pours over me when I hear the news, as this means I can now spend as much time as I want by her side, holding her hand and giving her the hugs I desire.

These shifts are a reminder of the truth that we do not live in a vacuum. Taking even a small step to reclaim our power can cause our environment to shift in unexpected ways. This is the reality of living in an interconnected world. Of course, walking in our power does not mean we will always get what our hearts desire. This is magical thinking, and ignores the fact that the best divine outcome for us in any given situation may not be the same as what we think we want. Embracing our personal power simply means deciding to walk in strength and capability, knowing that our choices and how we show up in the world influence what possibilities arise. Taking steps forward aids our ability to recognize the solutions flowing toward us that we might otherwise miss.

I had a meaningful time visiting my mom and seeing her in the comfort of her home (instead of navigating restrictive visiting guidelines with masks and no touching allowed). But even if her return home had not been made possible, the important thing was for me *to step into my own power to create a meaningful goodbye, no matter the circumstances.* In the seemingly hopeless and most difficult situations, we often forget our own ability to rise. But this is the one thing we must not do. It is when things are darkest that our own strength tends to surprise us.

We cannot control what events in the world transpire or what comes to pass as a result, but we can always choose what actions we will take in response. We exert our influence by taking a positive step forward, anchoring ourselves in hope, faith, and possibility. We choose to show up, trusting our inner strength and vision to light the way.

REFLECTIONS

- *Can you think of a time in your life when you stepped into your personal power? What did this look like?*
- *Have you ever confused trying to control an outcome with your ability to rise and take a proactive step forward, regardless of the results?*
- *Where in your life do you need to take a step forward in hope, faith, and possibility?*

45

DETOURS

Side roads are a path of discovery. They allow
us to grow in new and unexpected ways...
—JOURNAL ENTRY, DECEMBER 8, 2017

My friend recounted to me her trip to the monthly farmer's market yesterday. She went with only five items on her list and expected to be in and out in no time. However, the vendor for the first item she wanted to purchase had run out of what she needed. And the farmer who sold her second item wasn't there. In the middle of the market was a tiny store that usually carried the other three items. But when she arrived, she discovered that the store had recently closed, permanently.

As she shared with me her irritation at leaving the market empty-handed, or at least, without any of the items she'd wanted to check off her list, I thought about how seemingly little things have such a knack for getting under our skin when they go awry. It paralleled my circuitous cab ride home the other day. As my driver maneuvered the city streets, we came across multiple detour signs. Our intended route was thwarted left and right, and of course, this added a lot of time to what should have been a quick trip. The more detours we encountered, the more impatient I grew.

However, my cabdriver was as calm as could be and exuded an easygoing air. He didn't bat an eye or show any apparent sign of frustration as he meandered slowly through the streets, seeking to get back on track. Getting rerouted in life is part and parcel of human existence. But it is rare to find those souls who respond to life's detours with patience and a go-with-the-flow mentality. Or, even more rarely, with cheer. I was impressed with my cabdriver's positive demeanor and thought how I would like to be like him the next time I face an impasse that throws me off my intended course.

When life's details don't go according to plan, we have an opportunity to take a break from a linear mindset— an invitation to loosen our grip and our expectations. In doing so, we might relinquish something we don't actually need—attachment to a particular outcome, efficiency, checking tasks off a to-do list, or our own illusion of control. We grow more at ease with events unfolding in a direction other than anticipated. And best of all, we may find that our internal surrender leads to an unexpected gift of peace.

REFLECTIONS

- *How do you find yourself reacting when things don't go as planned?*

- *How can you use life's detours as a practice in letting go?*

46

FINDING RENEWAL IN RETREAT

*In order to understand the world, one has
to turn away from it on occasion.*
—ALBERT CAMUS

One of my favorite things to do is take a personal retreat. Although I only manage to do these retreats at best once a year, I really should do them more often. They are hugely instrumental in bringing grounding and refreshment and I always come away with a clearer lens through which to view the world.

My most recent retreat was in the early stages of the COVID-19 pandemic, shortly after quarantining requirements had lifted. I debated whether I should do one at all, as I usually drive to a different location for a few days. Doing so in this season felt somewhat risky. But as I considered that I was planning to be alone the entire time, it didn't feel that much different than being alone at home. I began to pack, eagerly anticipating a few days to re-center, still my spirit, and listen for guidance regarding present and future steps.

Even if you don't currently have the opportunity to leave your responsibilities for a day or two, there is tremendous value in withdrawing from our overly stimulated world, no matter how briefly. *There is power in retreat.* It gives us space to unhook from external forces for a while—daily distractions, the weight of the news cycle, other people's voices, and the viral fear that has become a constant companion in these times.

Too often, instead of living guided lives, we live reactive lives. Every day a single glance at the headlines gives us a multitude of things to react to, and anxiety and unrest fill our spirits. Unhooking provides us with a chance to leave these emotions behind and take a few steps back, helping us to regain clarity and vision. Letting go of the outside world in whatever way we can allows our attention to draw inward. Doreen Virtue describes this process so well: "I remember to breathe throughout the day. I remind myself that I can choose peace, no matter what is going on around me. Whenever I desire, I can retreat to that quiet place within simply by closing my eyes."

When I relocated to Mexico in 2018, many people asked me if I moved because of Trump's presidency (for the record, the answer is no). This question always struck me as odd, because I have never been inclined to make decisions that are simply reactions to what is going on around me. Instead, I've chosen to navigate my way through life from a place of purpose and guidance. This kind of knowing isn't dependent on pandemics, unrest, which people are elected, or which institutions crumble. It is an internal GPS that serves as a mooring in turbulent times. This is both the power and the fruit of anchoring ourselves in a higher vibration—we are not as easily buffeted by the waves of the planet.

Life's waves, of course, are inevitable. Still, it behooves us to take a break from the external stimuli that can easily cloud our thinking, and then trust and expect that whispers of guidance will come. Retreating gives us the gift of newfound strength. As we get our bearings again, we gain the needed perspective to cocreate a more elevated world. We see more clearly what our highest purpose is on the planet. And we are better equipped to respond to the challenges of our times.

REFLECTIONS

- *In what ways can you incorporate moments of retreat into your daily life?*
- *How does withdrawing give you needed perspective on our world's challenges?*

47

JOY IN "WHAT IS"

Whatever arises, love that.
—MATT KAHN

We climb the ancient stone steps of the 17th-century church, reaching the balcony that overlooks the orchestra and choir below. I am excited because we are coming to hear the complete rendition of Handel's *Messiah,* and it has been decades since I listened to the entire work. But upon reaching the balcony seating area, to my disappointment, there are only a few black folding chairs, some bleacher-style benches with no backs, and absolutely no view of the orchestra and choir below.

We are pointed to the bleacher seating, and as we sit down on the cold metal bench, all we can see are people's bodies in front of us. No one can glimpse the actual concert, except for a few people in the very first row of black folding chairs who attempt to peer through the wooden slats of the balcony railing. There is a blurry video projection of the orchestra and the singers on the wall to our immediate left. But not only is it out of focus, to watch it, we have to turn our heads at a 90-degree angle while our bodies remain facing forward.

At the prospect of sitting like this for three hours, I begin grumbling to my husband about the balcony seats being false advertising. And how could they sell "seating" in a place where we are unable to view the concert we've just paid for?

However, if there is one thing I've learned from living in another country, it's that you either roll with things or quite quickly die of frustration. Standards are different, as are expectations.

So, after grumbling for another ten minutes, I finally let myself listen to the beautiful music the orchestra has begun playing. I note the reactions of others in the same seating predicament as us, most of whom seem to be accepting the situation for what it is. Some sit with their eyes closed and focus on listening instead of straining to see something out of sight. Others choose to look at the blurry video projection, craning their necks at an odd angle, settling for at least a fuzzy glimpse of the action below.

As the music progresses, one anointed chorus after the next, I realize I can either continue to be grumpy and miss out on Handel's work of art, or I can let the music overtake me and relish in the amazing acoustics of this ancient church. Handel was a genius, after all. And as each chorus is sung, I am reminded again of the extreme beauty of this musical masterpiece. The challenge before me is the age-old struggle of *what is* and *what is not,* and I will myself to focus on *what is.*

Slowly, I begin to absorb the notes into every fiber of my being. I let myself remember my years in high school choir, performing this piece with the school orchestra every December for an auditorium full of people. Right before the "Hallelujah" chorus rolls around, I stand up in anticipation and feel moved as others around me stand as well. Handel's music fills the cavernous space of the church, and thunderous applause echoes in appreciation.

My experience of the concert could so easily have gone a different way. But the music had won, overcoming and subduing my inner struggle; it had captured my spirit and raised it to a higher plane.

Sometimes, the simplest choices of where to point our focus are the hardest. But as we allow ourselves to marinate with appreciation in the *what is* of our days, we have the power to alter every moment of our present.

REFLECTIONS

- *Where have you been focusing your attention of late?*
- *In what ways can you shift your focus from the tyranny of "what is not" to the gift of "what is"?*

48

RITUALS

A routine can begin to feel like a spiritual practice,
opening you to guidance, energy, and creativity.
Creating routines for yourself that comfort you
will quiet your mind, and it is this quiet mind
that allows inspiration to spring forth.
—JULIA CAMERON

Never underestimate the power of rituals. What may seem small and insignificant at first glance is a vital part of our creative expression. On any single day, these efforts might not appear to carry much weight. But it is the compilation of days and repeated efforts that pave the way for our creative ideas to be born.

This spring morning, I am reminded anew of the value of my daily writing ritual. It always begins with a cup of tea. This gives me time to settle in, to grow still. To let the noise in my head dissipate. I sit by my window and sip slowly, letting my eyes gaze at the flowering vine blooming on the courtyard wall. As my head clears, I can start to listen. I put my fingers to the keyboard and begin to explore a new direction or revisit the notes where I left off yesterday. I see with fresh eyes what is asking to be added or what needs to be reworked.

This meditative ritual allows me to create. It is a supportive practice that aids me in releasing my writing into the world. And it embodies the essence of the sacred. As I write this, I can hear local townspeople singing hymns in Spanish a few doors down. It is Sunday morning, and the church bells have been ringing to call them to gather. I know that my own divine ritual, allowing words to pour forth, is no different from the church's. It is just a different expression and a different container. The Spirit that illuminates them both is the same.

We add fuel to our creative work by reminding ourselves often of the power of our rituals. They have the capacity to transform not only others, through what we create, but also ourselves. These small acts may not always feel that important on any given day, but we are well-served to prioritize them. It is from these seemingly minor moments that the seeds of our creative gifts begin to blossom.

REFLECTIONS

- *What rituals aid you in your creative process?*
- *In what ways can you make them a more integral part of your work?*

49

SEEING CLEARLY

It is only with the heart that one can see rightly.
What is essential is invisible to the eye.
—ANTOINE DE SAINT-EXUPERY

Although Mexico has less material wealth than the United States, I have experienced greater heart fulfillment here than I ever did back home. Life is celebrated regularly, and I've found myself the recipient of incredible generosity, from both expats and Mexicans alike. It's almost like generosity is a way of life, instead of a single act or gift that is only given on occasion.

This past week a pre-Easter procession filled the town's streets in the early morning hours, as pilgrims who had been walking all night from a neighboring village made their way into San Miguel. Colorful flags and flowers arched over the cobblestone streets, and men, women, and children carried candlelit torches in the pre-dawn air. Townspeople lined the streets to watch and set out tables in front of their homes with a bounty of hot drinks and food for the weary travelers. This act of generosity and hospitality touched my spirit and deposited something profound within me.

Over the years, I have repeatedly observed that those with fewer material resources often enjoy richer lives—things like a more meaningful connection to one another, to Spirit, and to the stuff of life that truly matters. And in this, they are great teachers for the rest of us. But sadly, those of us who grow up amidst material wealth are not trained to look at the world this way. We've been taught to see those the world designates as "poor" as people to assist and be charitable toward, but not as people who possess true prosperity. However, the world offers us teachers in unexpected places, who can prompt us toward needed shifts in our priorities. For we need help in seeing clearly again.

I recently read a blog post about Silicon Valley, an epicenter of material wealth. The author grew up in the Valley and works at Google, and so she wrote from relevant life experience. She described the degree of soullessness she felt in her environment, and recounted the rampant mental health issues that plagued so many of her high school peers in her youth, even though they had access to every resource imaginable.

In contrast, living in Mexico regularly reminds me that inner fulfillment is entirely unrelated to material wealth. The more time I spend away from places brimming with surplus, the more I recognize the correlation between outer excess and inner lack. Poverty is not just a physical ailment; it is a spiritual one. Material wealth has a very real propensity to deaden our faculties and numb our souls. Those who live with less offer us a fresh vision. They help us reexamine our relationship with "more" and provide the clarity we need to choose a life that is lived in service to something other than its pursuit.

REFLECTIONS

- *When is your soul most fulfilled?*
- *Are these experiences in contrast to the cultural message that ties satisfaction to wealth?*
- *Who in your life might be an unlikely teacher modeling a countercultural experience of life satisfaction?*

50

SHOWING UP ANYWAY

Be messy and complicated and
afraid and show up anyway.
—GLENNON DOYLE MELTON

This past month I've been struggling mightily to put words on the page. This is a potential problem for a writer, or so my logical mind attempts to convince me. Every time I show up at the screen, my mind is a complete blank. "Show up anyway," my non-logical mind says. Even for twenty minutes, ten minutes, five minutes. Show up anyway. See what happens when I allow myself to enter that creative space without anything external drawing me in. Notice what emerges when I look at the state of my heart, *as it is,* no modification needed.

Ah. Maybe that's it. How easily we fall into the trap of thinking that we must either change ourselves, or arrive at a certain place, or somehow feel differently than we do before we create our best work. Perhaps it is possible for our work to emerge from those places that feel empty or dry. Sometimes a spark lies beneath the surface of these barren spaces, waiting to be ignited and cast a faint glow over a new trail to follow. And following this trail may just result in an offering that will resonate with others, as they too know what it is to have difficult days.

When we give ourselves permission to begin our work in an off-mood or under less-than-ideal circumstances, we practice a form of self-love. We make the decision to embrace who we are in the moment, declaring ourselves and it to be "okay." We no longer demand that our emotions change shape or that our circumstances be more accommodating of our work. We have faith that who we are, despite any particular lack we feel, is sufficient.

So show up, I will. No great mood, grand inspiration, or external reward beckoning me forth. But I know enough by now to believe that I must trust in the process. I must trust in the sheer act of being present, regardless of how much I protest in anticipation. I know that returning to my creative work has tremendous power to set things in motion and to shift my perspective. It will replenish me from the inside out. And although some days it may feel like we are simply showing up to give, our creativity, at its most profound level, is an exchange. It has the power to fill our well even as we empty it out. It will feed us as we feed it.

Today, I encourage you to engage with your creative desires, no matter how much resistance you may be battling. Remember that the practice of doing your work is an act of self-love. When you take steps to honor who you are, you affirm that what you have to give to the world is valuable. Try taking a step toward your creativity, *just as you are*, and see what happens. Extend radical acceptance to yourself. And maybe, just maybe, you'll find that your muse was waiting there all along—waiting to whisper a spark of something new.

REFLECTIONS

- *Do you find yourself postponing your creative work until you feel a certain way or the conditions are "right"? What might happen if you showed up anyway?*
- *Believe that engaging with your creativity, regardless of circumstance, is an act of self-love. Does this belief shift anything for you?*

51

SMALL THINGS

Each day comes bearing its own gifts.
Untie the ribbons.
—RUTH ANN SCHABACKER

Today I wake up and, after a week of being housebound, can finally go for a walk. I injured my back recently (by apparently doing nothing, which is surely a sign of getting old) and haven't been able to move around easily for days. But this morning my back shows signs of returning to normal, and I happily don my exercise clothes to take an early morning walk.

Taking a walk in Mexico is always full of fascinating sights and sounds—one's senses are filled to the brim with color, life, and warmth. I decide to purchase some roses from an elderly man I've passed numerous times before. Every morning he sits on the curb next to a table laden with roses in all different colors—red, yellow, pink, and white. He is slightly hunched over and there is a woman beside him, perhaps his wife or a family member. He always greets passersby with a smile.

After making my rounds to the local produce store and panadería, I approach his stand with a "Buenos días" and ask how much for a dozen roses. "Cincuenta," he tells me, and as I fumble through my change, I realize I don't have quite enough for a dozen and ask for seis instead. "Claro," he says as he stands up slowly and begins to select six roses one by one, carefully placing them together with some strands of baby's breath. He slips them into a plastic sleeve with his gnarled and arthritic hands, and then cuts a piece of red ribbon haltingly, tying everything together.

"Aquí tiene," he says, as he hands them to me with care, "muchísimas gracias." I thank him in return and wish him a good day as I set off toward home. As I walk up the street, my soul is full and I realize that this interaction has deposited a wealth of abundance within me. I feel gratitude for him, for the exchange, and for the awareness that the essence of life boils down to the simplest of acts. In them, we find some of the greatest gifts.

As I reach my house, I decide I will buy roses from him every week. It is the small things that shift our perspective on life and never fail to put what looms large in its proper place. For this, I am thankful.

REFLECTIONS

- *Make a list of 5–10 small things that have filled you with joy this week.*
- *In what ways does focusing on life's small gifts shift your perspective?*

52

LESSONS IN THE DARKNESS

If you spend enough time in the desert,
you will hear it speak.
—NNEDI OKORAFOR

One of my favorite places to go is the Jardín Botánico just outside of town. There are miles of trails leading through a semi-arid landscape, along canyon edges, and beside a placid lake. During the rainy season, this lake is full, and the excess water turns into waterfalls that cascade down a rocky ravine.

A friend recently warned me that when the dry season comes, the lake evaporates entirely. I had a hard time envisioning the lake completely gone, but this was certainly not welcome news. Sitting by a body of water has long been one of my restorative pastimes.

Sure enough, when I visit the gardens a month later, dry, cracked earth stares back at me where the lake had been—a vast sea of brown clay. It uncannily mirrors how my own soul has been feeling of late—dry and barren, with some cracks starting to show. The emptiness of the lake bed feels oddly familiar, as if the disappearance of the lake is a metaphor for the deconstruction I am experiencing in my own soul. I decide to sit with this awareness for a while. I listen. And I wonder what lessons the dried-up lake might have in store for me.

Then a few weeks later, a surprising thing happens. Green begins to spread across the dusty earth, covering the ground where the lake had once been. I marvel at this, wondering how a growing plant could spring into existence with no visible water source. It feels like a meadow of promise—the cracked earth literally offering up new life.

And then I realize, here is my lesson. *Barrenness is not a prelude to more barrenness.* It is, instead, something we must journey through, and even be willing to linger in, before something new is born. As Stephen Buhner writes, when we continually try to look on the bright side, it "interferes with our finding the wisdom that lies in the fruitful darkness." Desolate places in our own hearts have an invitation for us if we are willing to enter into them and listen. When we rush through these places in search of the sun, we miss the valuable lessons that only come when our souls have been laid bare.

As I gaze at the lake bed, the different shades of green gaze back, reminding me that they would not exist without the desolate stretch of brown clay. They whisper to my soul the truth that deconstruction is not without purpose. Author and theologian Barbara Brown Taylor writes: "I have learned things in the dark that I could never have learned in the light, things that have saved my life over and over again so that there is really only one logical conclusion. I need darkness as much as I need light."

May we find solace in knowing that darkness is one of life's many teachers. We need not fear it, but instead simply receive its lessons as we pass through, knowing that new life awaits us on the other side.

REFLECTIONS

- *What areas of your life feel most bleak or barren?*
- *What lessons might the darkness be trying to teach you?*

53

THE UNRESOLVED

*Be patient toward all that is unsolved in your heart
and try to love the questions themselves...*
—RILKE

Life as an expat isn't always easy, particularly in a country
that is less organized and less efficient than the States.
Although proponents of travel will tell glamorized tales
of adventure, the mere basics required to accomplish
day-to-day life tasks are a challenge in many places.

This is true many times over living in a small Mexican
town. The other week I ordered a rug on Amazon. I
received a notice saying it would come the following
week, so I made plans to be home the day of the delivery.
(Packages aren't left at the door due to theft, so one must
be at home to receive anything ordered.) The delivery day
comes and goes with no rug. FedEx, the carrier Amazon
used, indicates they will try again tomorrow. No rug
appears the next day, so I contact Amazon to try and
resolve the situation.

In the meantime, FedEx (known for being notori-
ously unreliable in Mexico) claims they have the wrong
address. This is quite odd, given the only address they

have access to is from Amazon, which has the correct information. Discussions ensue, and I am asked to give extra details about the delivery location (the color of the door, the house, etc.). Then, communications go silent for a period. Perplexed, I try calling FedEx a few days later. After multiple attempts, I finally get through to someone. However, they are unable to find any information associated with my tracking number.

After several more phone calls and following up with Amazon multiple times, the rug finally makes it to our house a month later. But not without plenty of tension and time spent trying to fix a problem that, in my American perspective, shouldn't have required nearly so much effort.

While in the overall scheme of things, a delayed rug delivery is very much a "first world problem," it nevertheless serves as an example of living with the tension of the *unresolved*. Like it or not, life has a way of offering us plenty of unresolved circumstances—from a simply less-than-ideal situation to a difficult pain or longing in our lives that has yet to be remedied.

How do we respond to what is unanswered in our lives? How do we react to what is not yet fulfilled? Maybe we decide to keep our fists clenched and attempt to bring desired resolutions by sheer force or strength of will. Or perhaps we expend large amounts of worry, thinking that our anxiety might eventually result in a longed-for shift. Or maybe we succumb to cynicism, believing it will protect our hearts from the pain of a hope deferred.

However, there is a more freeing option, one that would invite us to receive tension as a gift in disguise—a doorway to liberty. For anything that is unfinished or not at peace in our lives has the potential to deposit something transformative within us. Unresolved places highlight exactly how we are being triggered, and by what. They reveal the beliefs that still control us—those things that keep us dependent on external circumstances for our well-being. And without this felt tension, we would remain unaware of these unfree places in our hearts.

This realization helps us coexist more easily with what is not yet righted in our lives, letting go of some of our resistance. While we can still hope that our concerns will be righted in due time, we are better equipped to walk with what is unfinished and not prematurely escape our discomfort.

By welcoming tension as a gift, we allow it to transform all that is still bound within us. We release the inordinate expectations we hold of the future and reside more peacefully in the space that precedes it.

REFLECTIONS

- *Where is the "tension of the unresolved" showing up in your life these days?*
- *How can you allow it to be a gift that ushers in greater internal freedom?*
- *What beliefs are you being called to transform?*

54

STEADFASTNESS

*No tree can survive and grow without
nurturing and anchoring roots.*
—SIMON JACOBSON

Disposability is a trademark of our times. We see this not just in our material consumption, but also in our short-lived relationships with people, places, and work. We have become a culture obsessed with getting our needs met. Of course, there is nothing inherently wrong with identifying a need and satiating it. But this growing over-emphasis on self is quite the opposite of sustained devotion to something outside of ourselves. The "me" culture seems to be growing ever more entrenched, and true steadfastness, particularly when it costs us something, is becoming an outdated hallmark of the past.

The ability to be unwavering reveals itself most readily in times of crisis. Whether in the face of turbulence in our environment or community, our personal relationships, or at work, committing to someone, something, or somewhere is a rare commodity. Often our first response in a dire situation is, well, it must be time to leave. I will exit for greener pastures. Change is the only constant, right?

What would happen if, instead, we tried looking at storms and times of hardship as opportunities to lower our anchor and settle in? How would this shift our very experience of the storm itself, as well as our perception of our ability to embody perseverance and longevity?

There is a beauty to devotion that the world misses. When we choose to be unwavering, a stability enters our lives, callings, and relationships that brings many gifts. But we too often sell short the riches that emerge from longevity. We confuse consistent dedication with being limited, stuck, or trapped—instead of *embodied, rooted, and strong.*

Another way of saying this is that we value not giving up. A plant that is constantly being transferred from one pot to the next will never let its roots grow down entirely and reach its full size. If change is all it ever knows, its growth will remain stunted.

My parents recently celebrated 52 years of marriage. My mom has lived with Parkinson's for the past ten years and now requires round-the-clock care. Throughout the ups and downs of life, their union has depicted steadfast love lived out unconditionally over decades. Imperfect? Of course. But resolute in the midst of storms. This carries significance in an era where hardship thwarts the slightest of intentions.

If nothing else, this chapter is intended to raise a banner for a return to the kind of commitment that signifies an ability to stick with life, even when it's hard. It is a call to value longevity of presence (to a place, thing, calling, or person) as much as we value change and newness. We must learn to let our hearts root down in whatever soil we find ourselves, for only then will we get to witness the full expansion of its yet-unrealized potential. Only then will we glimpse the jewels that surface 10, 20, or 30 miles down the road of any pursuit and are not visible in the first few steps.

In the midst of storms, the lure of change is but one side of the proverbial coin. Let's not miss the oft-overlooked flip side of letting our roots grow deep… and experiencing the gains that only come from an unwavering devotion.

REFLECTIONS

- *What benefits have you experienced from lowering your anchor and settling in for the long haul, whether in a location, life calling, relationship, or career?*
- *Where have you found value in not giving up?*

55

WALKING IN FAITH

*Artists are visionaries. We routinely practice a form of
faith, seeing clearly and moving toward a creative goal
that shimmers in the distance—often visible
to us, but invisible to those around us.*
—JULIA CAMERON

I received an email last week from an artist friend of mine. She recently moved back to her hometown to pursue a photography project that's been brewing within her for months. She had spent the last year traveling and making her art along the way. Now she needed to return to her photography equipment and studio to properly execute the large-scale project that was asking to be birthed.

The call to this creative project required my friend to make a change in where she was living. Others of us might not need a geographic move, just the willingness to begin anew on a project we have put aside or discarded. Or maybe we simply need to be okay with not knowing where a current project is heading and commit to it anyway.

At the end of the day, all creative pursuits are ultimately about trusting the path. My friend's return to her hometown was the next step that made sense for her. Another friend is choosing to leave her business career to pursue her creative passions for the first time. I am leaving the art world behind and following the trail of a writing career because that is where the signs of creative life are pointing.

And that's just it. Our creative work does, in fact, call to us, giving us signs and guiding us forward. But we never get the whole road map all at once. Only a next step. And then one more. We really can never see much farther than a few feet ahead. And so, we must trust. Trust that the creation calling to us knows what it wants to become. Trust that we are chosen conduits able to birth the message given to us. Trust that in walking the path, each step we take honors what is asking to be born.

REFLECTIONS

- *What is the next step calling to you in your creative work?*
- *Give yourself permission to move forward, even if the bigger picture is hidden from sight.*

56

INVITING SURRENDER

It all falls into place in the moment of surrender,
that's when freedom and peace come and
take over your whole being.
—MARIA ERVING

In writing this book, I faced the repeated challenge of allowing it to form organically. From the beginning, it had a very clear life of its own, and it was my job to partner with it and not force a contrived external agenda upon it. Of course, this is much easier said than done. Sometimes I slipped. I gave in to feelings of pressure—self-induced, mostly—to speed this project up. I felt tempted to force the completion date into sight and insist this organic progression get in line with my own timeline.

And in the process, I forgot. I forgot to surrender to both the slow unfolding of this work of art and the larger picture of life into which it was being birthed. For I do not create in isolation. I am part, as we all are, of a much larger whole. And surrender is a gift that helps us connect to this larger picture and stay in sync with our small piece, as it joins with the multitude of other pieces surrounding us.

Sometimes surrendering asks us to let go...to open our hands and release our anxiety, the future, other people, and the past. And other times we are invited to surrender "into" something, to consciously embrace a reality we'd otherwise not willingly enter into...the unknown, being in process, pain, or mystery. Surrender is never an easy companion, and so we put up walls of resistance. It grates against our illusions of control and our desire for life to transpire according to our plans.

But no matter how difficult it might be to enter into surrender, freedom is always waiting for us on the other side. The practice of letting go is one of life's most powerful tools because it moves us from a place of spinning our wheels to an experience of inner stillness. It is a vital companion on our journey toward peace. It diffuses falsely created pressure head on and tells it to take a hike, giving us permission to move with the larger flow of life.

We know that our limited views do not allow us to see what is around the corner. As much as we try, we cannot predict the future. Surrender helps us acknowledge these limits and accept the reality that we do not know the big picture. Although surrender sometimes feels like loss, it is actually what opens us up to all that is. It is the doorway that leads to a bigger field than we could have previously imagined.

When we allow our circumstances to shape us, just the way they are, we find freedom. What we perceive to be *in the way* transforms us by *becoming the way.* Surrender enables us to embrace ourselves and our lives as they are. It beckons us to take a big breath in and exhale, and to dwell fully in the space where all is okay.

REFLECTIONS

- *Identify a situation or circumstance in your life that is an invitation to surrender. What does surrender look like to you? How does it feel?*
- *Finish this sentence: "When I surrender. . ."*

57

VISIONING

When you are inspired by some great purpose or
extraordinary project, all your thoughts break
their bonds: your mind transcends limitations,
your consciousness expands in every direction,
and you find yourself in a new, great,
and wonderful world.

—PANTANJALI

I sit here this morning filled with gratitude. I'm on the top floor of our house overlooking the Mexican colonial town we currently call home. There is a breeze wafting through the large open window and a cup of hot coffee in my hands. A woman sweeps the rooftop of the house two doors down. From another direction, a dog barks and a man calls out, "¡Cállate!" (Quiet!), and once more, "¡Calla!" Flowering vines spill over an old stone wall adjoining the neighboring church, its steeple glimmering in the sunshine.

I pinch myself to take in the fullness of this morning's view and the reality of having established an international life outside of the U.S. This reality has been on my visioning board for six years. And before making it onto a tangible visioning board, it was a recurring thought for at least the past decade. This morning I am enjoying reflecting on just how this vision came about and celebrating its manifestation.

My husband and I have had a long-held wish to establish a life outside of the States. We have always enjoyed other cultures and places and carry within us a desire to travel and explore. Many of our friends are from other countries, and we have always felt at home in the world of expats.

But the details of how, where, and when eluded us for many years. And, while this vision was still in seed form, we could also sense that it wasn't the right season for it to come to fruition. So, knowing that dreams and visions take time to birth—and sometimes a very long time—we decided to hold the seeds and wait.

However, we did not wait passively. Despite our future's uncertainty, we stayed open to possibility and explored avenues when they arose. And, as best we could, we remained detached from specific outcomes. The exact how-tos of our international dream did not fully come into view until we made the explicit plan to move to Mexico in the summer of 2018. But even after moving, we only intended to stay in the country for six months. The unfolding of what is now a plan to remain longer-term was hidden from view.

When we envision what we most want to manifest, sometimes we place too tight a grip on the details of how it will all play out, attempting to force the exact outcome we desire. The challenge, then, becomes embracing a sense of possibility over and over again and holding everything quite loosely. Because despite our best efforts, we are unable to imagine the radical fullness of any particular vision. We can have aspirations, but often the Universe will have an even grander plan in mind, one we can't possibly visualize ahead of time. As a spiritual mentor once shared with me, "The greatness of who you are will extend beyond your wildest dreaming."

Nevertheless, our dreams are an excellent place to begin. In allowing ourselves the freedom to dream, we start to cultivate the seeds of our destinies. Visioning with open hands gives voice to our desires, helping us picture what being fully alive looks and feels like. It turns what could be an otherwise stagnant life into one where dreams and hopes are seen, nurtured, and honored. When we vision, we partner with the Universe and say, "Let's go on this great adventure together!" The outcome is unknown. Yet when we stay open to what *could be* and release the limits of our thinking, beautiful surprises await us.

REFLECTIONS

- *What dream are you excited to move toward? What is one exploratory step you can take?*
- *Practice believing in the greatness of your vision while simultaneously releasing your attachment to how and when it will manifest.*

CONCLUSION

I want to close with a word of encouragement. Creating our work and the lives we desire is no easy feat. Life is messy, complicated, and if nothing else, a ready supply of challenges. But at the same time, it is an experience of beauty, hope, and possibility. And it is these qualities I have tried to bring forth through the previous pages.

The creative process is not just about crafting the work unique to your particular calling. It is ultimately about entering into and creating the life you are destined to live. And more often than not, it is about living larger lives than we ever thought possible. My hope is that you come away with inspiration to go after the life calling to you and a renewed sense that you have the power to act as an agent of change in your own story.

For this book is ultimately about transformation. In becoming acute observers of our own lives and surroundings, letting what we see and experience touch us at a deep level, we open up to change. This is the simple yet profound act of allowing our lives to be altered by the ordinary. The things we are most prone to overlook are often our greatest teachers. As we grow in our awareness, we are repeatedly led from places of struggle to places of renewal and metamorphosis.

Socrates is quoted as saying, "The unexamined life is not worth living." I would add to this that as we become more aware, we become more awake. May you know that you have the power to transform not only your individual life, but also the lives of those around you. Our own growth has a ripple effect that always extends outward. May you find peace along the journey as you evolve into the fullness of who you are destined to be.

ACKNOWLEDGMENTS

It takes a multitude of people to birth a book, each with different gifts, and I am so grateful for all those who have lovingly contributed to this work. As inspirational teacher Claire Zammit says, "We do not become ourselves by ourselves." This is certainly true for an author's journey!

A very heartfelt thanks to: Anna Geller, the first one to view the content of this book and provide guidance with writing a book proposal; Sandie Sedgbeer, my book coach and editor, who called out my larger writing voice and offered such valuable expertise, guidance, and nurturing support; Teja Watson, for her meticulous proofreading skills; and Jo Walker, for designing a truly beautiful cover.

To my early readers Rene, Mary, and Amy, thank you for giving me such valuable feedback and encouragement. Your support gave me the momentum to move this project from draft stage to a finished book. To Tabby Biddle—thank you from the bottom of my heart for calling forth the writer within me and providing loving containers of support for both this book and my first one. You are a true champion of women's voices!

Thank you to Catherine DeMonte, Deborah Moldow, Terry Persun, Melissa Cistaro, Amy Gottlieb, Colette Lafia, Rebecca Lefebvre and Rene Norman for offering such kind words of endorsement. And to my San Miguel de Allende writing group where this book had its beginnings—I am so grateful for all of the Wednesday mornings we wrote together in the Bellas Artes courtyard.

Finally, a heartfelt thanks to you, the reader. I truly hope this book benefitted your heart and soul. I invite you to drop me a line at karen@karenkinney.com and share your experience.

ABOUT THE AUTHOR

KAREN KINNEY is a writer, visual artist, and teacher. At her core, she is a mystic and guide, channeling wisdom through her creative work. Contemplative spiritual practice and inner transformation are the building blocks of her creative expression.

Her first book, *The Reluctant Artist: Navigating and Sustaining a Creative Path,* is a guide to fully owning and nurturing your creative passions. In addition to writing books, Karen is a freelance writer and her articles and essays have appeared in Common Dreams, Cultural Daily, A Loved Life, and Mexico News Daily.

She has pursued a multifaceted art career and her work resides in numerous private collections, including those of Stanford University, actor Bob Odenkirk, and NPR's Guy Raz. She has designed installation work for the Los Angeles International Airport and painted murals in Los Angeles and Mexico.

Karen has taught about creative freedom in the U.S., at the University of Hong Kong, and at the San Miguel de Allende International Writers' Conference in Mexico. She is also passionate about providing creative platforms for women's spiritual perspectives and experiences. She curates a quarterly newsletter on the divine feminine and writes about spirituality and transformation from a feminist perspective.

Karen resides in San Miguel de Allende, Mexico.

karenkinney.com
@karen_e_kinney
@karen_e_kinney
karen.kinney.4